A Therapist's Guide

Assisting Our LGBTQ+ Loved Ones

Richard Cohen, M.A.

PATH Press
Bowie, Maryland

© 2024 Richard Cohen, M.A.
PATH Press

All rights reserved. Reproduction or translation of any part of this work beyond that permitted by Section 107 or 108 of the 1976 United States Copyright Act without the permission of the copyright owner is unlawful. Requests for permission or further information should be addressed to the Permissions Department, PATH Press.

This publication is designed to provide accurate and authoritative information in regard to the subject matter covered. It is sold with the understanding that the publisher is not engaged in rendering legal, accounting, counseling or other professional service. If legal advice, counseling or other expert assistance is required, the services of a competent professional person should be sought. *From a Declaration of Principles jointly adopted by a committee of the American Bar Association and a committee of publishers.*

Without limiting the rights under copyright reserved above, no part of this publication may be reproduced, stored in or introduced into a retrieval system, or transmitted, in any form or by any means (electronic, mechanical, photocopying, recording or otherwise) without the prior written permission of the publisher of this book.

All rights reserved.
ISBN 979-8-9870260-9-0

Library of Congress Control Number: 2024905803

Cohen, Richard Alfred
October 1952

Cover design: Katarina / www.fiverr.com
Layout designer: Lisa DeSpain / www.book2bestseller.com

PATH Press
P.O. Box 2315
Bowie, MD 20718
Tel. 301-805-5155
www.pathinfo.org

Printed in the United States of America

Acknowledgements

I stand upon the shoulders of many great men and women who came before me. Personally I would like to thank Dr. Joseph Nicolosi Sr., Dr. Elizabeth Moberly, Dr. Robert Kronemeyer, Dr. Martha Welch, Dr. Charles Socarides, Dr. Dean Byrd, Dr. Richard Fitzgibbons, Dr. Irving Bieber, Dr. Mary Ainsworth, Dr. John Bowlby, and Father John Harvey. Their publications and presentations have enriched my life personally and professionally.

Thanks to my incomparable editors: Mary Hamm, Phillip Schanker, and Lily Oliveri. You are the best. I am deeply grateful for your invaluable assistance.

Thanks to my beautiful and faithful wife Jae Sook, and our three remarkable children: Jarish, Jessica and Alfred. I love you all with my life.

Thanks to my beloved pastors and friends: John & Trina Jenkins, Keith & Vicki Battle, Ron & Brenda Crawford, Alfred & Susie Owens, Anthony & Cynthia Moore and Bessie Hayes. I love you all so very much.

Thanks to my dear forever friend Caleb Brundidge. You are a marvelous man of God.

Thanks to John and Hilde Wiemann for your friendship and professional assistance.

> "The Spirit of the Lord God is upon me, because the Lord has anointed me to preach good tidings to the poor; He has sent me to heal the brokenhearted, to proclaim liberty to the captives, and the opening of the prison to *those who are bound*; ² To proclaim the acceptable year of the Lord, and the day of vengeance of our God; to comfort all who mourn, ³ To console those who mourn in Zion, to give them beauty for ashes, the oil of joy for mourning, the garment of praise for the spirit of heaviness; that they may be called trees of righteousness, the planting of the Lord, that He may be glorified."
>
> —Isaiah 61:1-3 (NKJV)

Table of Contents

Acknowledgments 3

Introduction 7

**PART I: Blueprint for Healing:
Four Stages of Resolving Unwanted
Same-Sex Attraction (SSA)** 13

    Simple Truths about Same-Sex Attraction (SSA) 29

    Meaning Behind Same-Sex Attraction (SSA) 36

    Ten Potential Causes of SSA 49

    Seven Stages of "Coming Out" 66

    How to Assist Those Who Experience Unwanted SSA 71

    Four Stages of Resolving Unwanted SSA 79

    Need for Healthy Touch in the Healing Process 122

**PART II: Blueprint for Assisting Families
and Friends with SSA Loved Ones:
Twelve Principles for Change** 131

    Introduction 132

    Syllabus for a Parents Support Group 141

Summary of the Key Points from
　　Gay Children, Straight Parents 152
Two Stories from Parents who
　　Participated in our Classes 153

Conclusion 165

Resources 177

Organizations 179

About the Author 181

Please note: I use the term "gay" throughout the book as a socio-political term denoting someone who has accepted their Same-Sex Attraction (SSA) and decides to live a homosexual life. Also, the term LGBTQ+ (Lesbian, Gay, Bisexual, Transgender and Queer/Questioning+) is used for socio-political purposes. I do not believe there is any such thing as a "homosexual" person (viewed as a noun). There are only people who experience SSA (viewed as an adjective, describing someone's thoughts, feelings, and/or desires).

Introduction

I love the entire Lesbian, Gay, Bisexual, Transgender, Queer+ (LGBTQ+) community. I respect the client's right of self-determination to follow the path of love that brings him or her the greatest joy. I believe Same-Sex Attraction (SSA) is not about SSA. Ultimately, it is about hurts in the heart that have not healed, and legitimate needs for love that have never been experienced in the critical ages and stages of child development. Therefore, SSA is not about sex but the psyche's attempt to heal and grow into the fullness of one's masculinity or femininity.

From the 1970s to the mid-1980s, I was the client who desperately sought help to resolve my unwanted same-sex attraction (SSA). Most therapists had no clue how to help me. After my breakthrough in 1987, I went back to graduate school for a Master of Art's degree in counseling psychology. From 1989, I became the psychotherapist helping hundreds of men and women find freedom from unwanted SSA, ultimately fulfilling their heterosexual dreams. I know personally and professionally that change *is* possible.

> "Dear God. Please take away my homosexual feelings. I never asked for them. Why won't you take them away?"

I prayed this prayer day after day, month after month, and year after year from elementary school to my undergraduate years at Boston University. But God never took them away. At the same time, I had a dream to marry a woman and create a beautiful family.

In 1970 I came out as a gay man in my senior year of High School. My parents swiftly sent me to a psychiatrist who had absolutely no idea how to help me. Off to Boston University I went. There I had several boyfriends in my freshman year, and a partner for the next three years. I grew up outside of Philadelphia in a Jewish family. My boyfriend Kurt loved Jesus. Because I loved Kurt, I wanted to understand about this Jesus, so I read the New Testament for the first time in my life. It was amazing. I fell in love with Christ. He was congruent on the inside and outside, and he offered grace, forgiveness and love.

I became a believer and prayed to the Lord, "Please take away my unwanted same-sex attractions," but still they persisted. While reading Scripture, Kurt and I realized that we were not supposed to be having sex, and we broke off our relationship.

INTRODUCTION

For the next nine years I lived as a celibate man. During this time, I met my wife-to-be, Jae Sook, who hailed from Korea. I told her about my past. She was completely loving and accepting. And yet, after we married my homosexual feelings returned. It became a living nightmare.

I hit the floor in prayer: "Why didn't you take these desires away? I did everything you asked of me. I was a good Christian man." Back into therapy I went and one-by-one the causes of my SSA were revealed:

1) Lack of bonding with my father
2) Overattachment to my mother
3) Physical abuse by my older brother
4) Sexual abuse by my Uncle Phil when I was five years old

As I began to work through the pains of my past, my same-sex attractions diminished. Finally, in the arms of a dear friend, who just happened to also be named Phillip, I grieved the core pain of my sexual abuse and the hurts I incurred from my father and older brother. There I discovered the secret to freedom—when my broken heart was heard and healed, while being held by a healthy heterosexual man, my homosexual feelings no longer had a purpose in my life.

After my breakthrough, I prayed to God, "What would you have me do now?" In 1987 I received my calling: help others who experience unwanted SSA, assist their family members and friends, and teach the world the truth about homosexuality. I went to graduate school and received my Master of Arts (M.A.) degree in counseling psychology, and for the past 35 years as a psychotherapist, I have had the honor of assisting thousands worldwide who experience unwanted SSA in fulfilling their heterosexual dreams, helped hundreds of parents in reconciling with their LGBTQ+ loved ones, and trained over 6,000 professional therapists and ministry leaders how to love and understand those who wrestle with their sexual orientation and gender identity.

I am neither homophobic nor anti-gay. Once again, I love the entire LGBTQ+ community and respect each individual's right to choose his or her own path. Today my beautiful wife and I have been married for 44 years, and we have three amazing adult children. My dream came true. I know personally, professionally and scientifically that people are not essentially born with same-sex attraction, that no one chooses to have SSA, and that change *is* possible!

Many of your clients are looking to you for help, hope, and a path that will allow them to resolve their unwanted Same-Sex Attraction (SSA). It is essential that you educate yourself about the basic causes of SSA as well as a plan for healing/resolving their unwanted desires. Additionally, their family members and friends will also seek your guidance. I will offer you practical tools to assist both of these populations.

- First, I have developed a four-stage protocol for assisting those who experience unwanted SSA as detailed in *Being Gay: Nature, Nurture or Both*?
- Second, I have authored a 12-step protocol for parents, family members, friends, and the religious community as outlined in *Gay Children, Straight Parents: A Plan for Family Healing*.
- Third, I have created a protocol for therapists, counselors, coaches and ministry leaders detailed in our *Clinician's Handbook: Assisting Our LGBTQ+ Loved Ones and Film Series*.

The majority of SSA strugglers, those who have LGBTQ+ loved ones, therapists and ministry leaders are ignorant about these solutions and the potential for real and lasting change. I therefore want to share with you in this book (and further detailed in the other three publications) the truth, the gold that I have mined from my personal and professional journey:

- Struggler: I experienced unwanted SSA from the time I was in elementary school. It was extremely painful not understanding why I experienced homosexual desires or how to resolve them.
- Overcomer: It was a long and painful journey to figure out why I experienced SSA, and it took even longer to heal the wounds that created those desires in the first place. Today, I stand as a victor of love. I have been married to my wonderful wife

Jae Sook since 1980, and we have three incredible adult children.
- Healer: For thirty-five years as a psychotherapist and sexual orientation and gender identity specialist, I have helped hundreds of men and women who experienced unwanted SSA fulfill their heterosexual potential, helped hundreds of parents restore relationships with their SSA children, and helped thousands of others through our healing seminars and online classes.
- Educator: I have taught thousands of therapists, counselors, coaches, ministry leaders and the general public about the causes of SSA and a successful treatment plan for change.

I have had the privilege of being on both sides of the therapist's couch—first as a client and now as a counselor. As in all professions, we bring our life experiences to our work. I am a healing artist. I know the "slings and arrows of outrageous fortune" that burden those living with unwanted same-sex attraction. I am a worthy journeyman. I can talk the talk because I have walked the walk. And it certainly was a "road less traveled."

My greatest desire is to shed light upon the truth of SSA, how to help those who seek change, and how to assist their loved ones. This book, and our *Clinician's Handbook: Assisting Our LGBTQ+ Loved Ones and Film series*, will equip you with the tools necessary to help both the struggler and his or her loved ones.

PART I

Blueprint for Healing: Four Stages of Resolving Unwanted Same-Sex Attraction (SSA)

In my book *Being Gay: Nature, Nurture or Both?*, you will learn about the ten potential causes of SSA and the four-stage model of healing. Every other chapter is a testimony of transformation from former clients who resolved their unwanted SSA; many of them are now married and have children. Changing one's sexual orientation and gender identity is possible, and this is documented through scientific research (please read Dr. James Phelan's book *Successful Outcomes of Sexual Orientation Change Efforts*, Phelan Consultants LLC, 2014).

Lessons learned over the past thirty-five years as a psychotherapist:

1—SSA is not about SSA or sex. It is a smoke screen for a hurting heart. Your client may come to you saying, "I don't want to be gay. I don't want to live a gay life. Please help me resolve these feelings and be strictly heterosexual." First, give him or her hope that change *is* possible. Next, you need to reframe their concept of being "gay" and being "heterosexual." They want to be rid of these unwanted feelings. However, these feelings are a message from their souls, trying to get their attention. SSA is not bad. SSA is not evil. SSA is not a curse from God or the Devil. SSA is the psyche's attempt to communicate that something is hurting inside, needs attention, resolution, and the right kinds of love.

It took years to develop SSA, therefore it will take time to resolve the issues that created those desires. In my clinical practice, the process of healing takes 1½ to 3 years. The amount of time it takes to resolve unwanted SSA is dependent upon *severity, sincerity and support:*

1) Severity of wounding experienced in childhood and adolescence.
2) Sincerity: effort that he/she is willing to invest in the healing process.
3) Support: number of healthy, heterosexual mentors and friends surrounding him or her will have a direct correlation to his or her growth into true

masculinity or true femininity. Without healthy, heterosexual mentors and friends, the SSA struggler may continuously sexualize normal needs for healthy bonding. As SSA is not about sex, growing into the fullness of their true gender identity will take time and investment from numerous healthy, heterosexual family members, friends, mentors and spiritual leaders.

2—Clients need to be assured that they don't need to "get rid" of their SSA. One former client, a tall, handsome physician said during the first session, "I want to get rid of my SSA, but at the same time, I'm afraid to lose it!" To which I replied, "It's OK. Your SSA has been your best friend for most of your life. Let's not focus on your SSA, because SSA is not about SSA." When they resolve the hurts of their past—the quiet forms or obvious manifestations of trauma that occurred in early childhood and/or adolescence—and experience healthy love from those of the same gender, SSA will naturally diminish and Opposite-Sex Attractions (OSA) will ensue. We are all biologically designed heterosexual—men and women fit perfectly together. Two men or two women do not.

3—If there is a dual diagnosis, or comorbidity, first you must help the client resolve the other issue(s), i.e., alcohol addiction, porn and masturbation addiction, substance abuse, etc. Unless they begin to resolve their addiction(s), he or she will continuously revert to this pattern of behavior when experiencing stress or pain and delay any possibility of healing. If the client is unable or unwilling to deal with his or her addiction(s), or other diagnosis, it is unprofessional of you to attempt to assist him or her. Once again, SSA is not about SSA. First things first.

4—Dr. Dean Byrd stated the following, "Be more than a therapist, and less than a parent." You are their cheerleader. Encourage your clients throughout their therapy, especially during their darkest days: "Never, ever give up. I know it hurts. I know you're in pain. Keep going, it will get better." Keep instilling hope in him and her. Keep them on the path of the four-stages of healing. Just "be there" for him when he feels so hopeless and discouraged (be a "sympathetic witness," as Dr. Alice Miller stated in her landmark book *The Drama of the Gifted Child*). Be their biggest cheerleader. Imbue hope in their outcome of fulfilling their dreams. "You can do it. I believe in you. I will be by your side. Never give up!" More than a therapist, less than a parent. Of course, you are not their "friend," although many clients will think of you in this way, as you are the first person who knows all of his or her deepest, darkest secrets, and still demonstrate unconditional regard, concern and care. SSA represents an attachment strain; therefore, maintaining an aloof demeanor is contra-indicated, as it will only foster a greater sense of detachment on the part of the client (thus, a traditional Freudian approach will only exacerbate their attachment issues). As for me, my clients always knew that I loved them, that I was always a safe harbor in the storms of life.

> "The emotionally detached therapist reactivates memories of earlier frustration from the cold and critical father. To correct this error, Moberly [he is referring to Dr. Elizabeth Moberly] explains that the therapist must be more emotionally involved and, within therapeutic guidelines, permit dependency. The therapist must be of the same sex as the client to allow him to work through developmental blocks with the same-sex parent" Joseph Nicolosi Sr., *Reparative Therapy of Male Homosexuality: A New Clinical Approach* (Northvale, NJ: Jason Aronson, Inc., 1991, Liberal Mind Publishers, updated edition, 2020), 20.

5—Time alone does not heal all wounds; it only buries them deeper. We need to help the client trace and face what occurred, grieve the losses of his or her past, and experience new and healthy love from those capable of giving. *One needs to be real and feel in order to heal.* It took years to develop SSA, therefore it will take time to resolve the hidden issues and fulfill unmet love needs in healthy relationships.

> "Unless a person can *feel* his emotions, he can't get to the root of his disturbance. The core of the

therapeutic problem is to free and then rechannel the energies that have been locked in the character armor and the muscular armor. To do this, it is necessary to bring to awareness and resolution the painful emotions that split the wholeness of the Self. The goal is a natural, healthy, and unified human being, free of pretense and deceit, whose interior matches his exterior" Robert Kronemeyer, *Overcoming Homosexuality* (New York City, NY: Macmillan Publishing Co., Inc., 1980), 113.

6—The wounds experienced in hurtful relationships must be healed in healthy relationships. We cannot heal on our own because all issues are relational. Grieving alone into one's pillow at night will not work. That kind of grief will become cyclical. Real love must be experienced in healthy relationships in order to heal old wounds. We need to share our truth, feel accepted, build trust, and then experience real love. Remember there are no quick fixes in the matters of the heart. Additionally, as the therapist or coach, you must, must, must help the client to build a strong Support Network. He needs healthy Opposite-Sex Attracted (OSA) men to be his friends and mentors. She needs the same, with OSA women. More about building the Support Network in *Being Gay*, Chapters Four and Six (pages 98–105, and 166–182).

Men coming out of unwanted SSA must first heal with other men, experience belonging and being one of the guys. Then, and only then, will he be ready to be a man with a woman. And the same holds true for women who experience unwanted SSA. She must first be a woman among women before being successful with a man. We must first experience a sense of our own gender identity and belonging to our own kind, before being secure enough to understand and love the opposite sex.

> "...we do not sexualize what we identify with; when we identify with someone, we are no longer sexually attracted to them. It is always to the other-than-ourselves that we are drawn" Joseph Nicolosi Sr., *Reparative Therapy of Male Homosexuality: A New Clinical Approach* (Northvale, NJ: Jason Aronson, Inc., 1991, Liberal Mind Publishers, updated edition, 2020), 186.

7—One needs to understand the opposite sex from one's own properly formed gender identity's point of view: After SSA men resolve their homo-emotional and/or homo-social issues (wounds with dad and other guys), and bonds with healthy OSA men, *then* they learn about women from a masculine perspective. Previously, most men who experience SSA viewed women from a female perspective, as they were more aligned with their mothers and/or girls during the critical ages and stages of child and adolescent development. Thus, they viewed the world of women from a more feminine point of view.

Now, as they think about dating and mating, they will learn about the world of women from a masculine perspective. Of course, the same healing process applies to women who experience SSA. They need to bond with healthy, heterosexual women and *then* learn about men from a female perspective. This is a process that cannot be omitted. More about this phenomenon in Chapters Four and Six in *Being Gay*.

8—It is imperative to let your client know that when stressed or under duress, his or her SSA may emerge as a coping mechanism. He has not regressed if he once again experiences SSA. It is merely the repetition of an old neurological pattern. The key is to understand that it is not about SSA, it is about dealing with the present situation and circumstances in healthy and effective ways (more about this in Chapters Four and Six of *Being Gay*). As soon as she or he takes good care of herself/himself, or perhaps recalls moments of being loved, then the vestiges of any past unhealthy pattern and SSA will fade away, and she or he will feel much better. Additionally, if someone experienced sexual abuse or other forms of same-sex activity at a young age, the brain's neural-pathways were formatted to experience SSA. Therefore, again, under stress a fallback response may be same-sex attraction. It only means that their brain is returning to old habits. One should breathe, relax, get in touch with one's own soul, and listen to what it is trying to communicate. When he or she does this, their SSA dissipates. For it is never about SSA (or sex), it is about proper self-care and learning to love and be loved. Once again, SSA is not about SSA or sex.

9—SSA is a gift to help him/her heal, grow, and become the man or woman he/she is truly meant to be. Over time, you may help him understand that the SSA he wrestles with, thinks is his burden, is actually his best friend. Embrace his SSA: listen to it, learn from it, and become a good steward of his soul. In the process of growth, he will become a more loving man. After that, he will bless others because he has journeyed through his own personal hell and returned a healthier man, capable of loving and offering his gifts to others. All the same applies to a woman who experiences unwanted SSA.

> "Sexual brokenness pinpoints the location of our past harm and highlights the current roadblocks that keep us from the freedom we desire. If we are willing to listen, our sexual struggles will have so much to teach us" Jay Stringer, *Unwanted: How Sexual Brokenness Reveals Our Way to Healing* (Carol Stream, IL: NavPress/Tyndale House Publishers, Inc., 2018), xix.

10—"You are not gay." "You are not a lesbian." "You are not a homosexual." "You are not bisexual." "You are not non-binary." "You are not transgender." "You *are* either a precious son or daughter of God. That is your true identity." If your client does not believe in God, simply assure him or her, "You are biologically designed as a man," or "You are biologically designed as a woman." This is so important to convey to your client at the outset of therapy. "Gay," "Lesbian," "Homosexual," "Bisexual," "Non-binary," "Transgender" are all man-made terms. They are inaccurate labels. In cultures throughout the world today, these terms are used as nouns, putting people in boxes. However, SSA is an adjective, describing someone's thoughts, feelings, and/or desires.

11—Never cry when your client is crying. You may already know this, however I learned it the hard way, through experience. During a session, a young woman was recalling past childhood sexual abuse. Naively, I began to silently cry, tears fell from my eyes. As soon as she saw me crying, she ceased grieving and stopped sharing. I learned that while a client is describing a painful memory of the past or present, and perhaps crying, it is never appropriate for the therapist to show any visible sign of emotion. Like those working in an Emergency Room of a hospital, they cannot show any powerful reaction to the malady of the patient, otherwise, the patient will become more upset or afraid. We too must show compassion while remaining detached, a very fine line to walk. In this way, the client will feel safe. If we empathize too much, the client may feel like she must take care of us, as she may have done so with her parent(s) or caregiver(s).

12—I have observed two different types of clients: 1) those who are **strong-willed** and are eager and capable of completing their homework assignments and developing a Support Network, and 2) those who are **weak-willed**, who do not do their homework, and are afraid of reaching out to others for support.

After establishing a trust relationship (which takes at least two-three months), I keep the client on track, demanding that she/he complete all of their homework assignments. If they did not do the homework required, there are a few alternative approaches: 1) do the homework assignment(s) during the session, or 2) the client finds a friend or accountability partner; they meet and do the homework assignments together.

My hypothesis about the weak-willed client is that during the second stage of development (separation-individuation), he or she was unable to successfully individuate from the maternal figure, and continued to be the "pleaser," good-little boy or good-little girl. Additionally, there may have been trauma(s) or painful experiences during these early stages of child development. Unable to express his or her own needs in a positive, assertive manner, the child was left in a state of fear and inability to actualize his/her own true personality. This may have resulted in a weak-willed individual.

13—Be careful with your precious time. Forgive me for being so blunt, however, I suggest working mostly with strong-willed clients. This may sound harsh: weak-willed clients may drain you, lean on you, require more of you, and after all is said and done, accuse you. Tell them that you are very sorry, but you are not capable of helping them. Do not blame them, as they already feel bad. Suggest they work with many of the online support groups, and/or refer them to another therapist (https://www.pathinfo.org/organizations).

14—There is no such thing as "Conversion Therapy" (CT). This is a term literally created by leaders of the LGBTQ+ (Lesbian, Gay, Bisexual, Transgender, Queer/Questioning+) movement, to make therapists who assist clients that experience unwanted SSA look homophobic, anti-gay and ill-informed. The inherent implication of the term "Conversion Therapy" is that we are trying to "convert" someone to our beliefs. The pejorative term of CT was not created within the therapeutic community, but by LGBTQ+ activists, as a socio-political catchphrase. Please allow me to illuminate the tremendous confusion and cleverness of the term "Conversion Therapy."

First of all, the implication is that therapists, or a variety of therapies and/or ministries, are attempting to "convert" the client to become heterosexual, often against his or her will. Nothing could be further from the truth. As therapists, we only assist those who experience unwanted SSA. Secondly, LGBTQ+ activists intentionally lumped together the good, the bad and the ugly: ex-gay ministries, counselors using horrifically antiquated methods, religiously-oriented programs, and finally, professionally trained therapists who use scientifically proven modalities. A simple online search of "Conversion Therapy" will result in a rainbow assortment of subjective definitions, based on an approximation of the person's or organizations' point of view. CT is not a scientific term founded upon years of research and confounding of evidence through scientifically, peer-reviewed studies. Stated quite simply, it is a political term coined by LGBTQ+ activists to denigrate well-trained therapists and those seeking to resolve their unwanted SSA through good therapy.

In my career, I have worked with many gay-identified clients who had no desire to change their sexual orientation. Of course, I worked primarily with clients who experienced unwanted SSA and sought change. I, and my colleagues, believe in the client's right of self-determination. We view this as their basic human right of autonomy. Once again, the pejorative term of CT was not created within the therapeutic community, but by LGBTQ+ activists, as a socio-political expression. For a more in-depth explanation about the LGBTQ+ movement and their terms, please read *Understanding Our LGBTQ+ Loved Ones* (Richard Cohen, Bowie, MD: PATH Press, 2022).

When I began my practice as a psychotherapist in the late 1980s, there was no such term as Conversion Therapy. It magically appeared in the early 2000s, launched by LGBTQ+ activists. Through repeating this term loud and long enough, it was deemed tried, tested and true. Media sources worldwide picked up on the CT term, and it grew legs as something legitimate. If the news outlets say it, it must be true. Abracadabra, another great tactic of LGBTQ+ activists, attempting to silence sincere clients who seek to resolve of their unwanted homosexual feelings, and the professionals who assist them.

15—Fetishes are not about fetishes. A fetish is not about the fetish or sex. There are always trauma origins of each fetish, e.g., feet, shoes, underwear, sadomasochism, cuckolding. As with SSA, we help the client understand the meaning behind his or her fetish(es). A warning: do not deal directly with the fetish of your client in the early stages of the healing process. Follow the four-stage protocol, and when the time is right (generally in Stage Three), address the profound meaning that created this manifestation. It always hides a hurting heart. Listen, learn, and patiently accept your client. Read Jay Stringer's book entitled *Unwanted: How Sexual Brokenness Reveals Our Way to Healing* (NavPress, ©2018).

16—Ideally, the client should seek therapy with someone of the same gender. Same-Sex Attraction represents an attachment strain with members of the same sex. Therefore, men who experience unwanted SSA would benefit most by working with a male therapist, and an SSA woman working with a female therapist. If there are no same-gender therapists available, then the counselor will help his or her client find same-gender mentors. Dr. Maria Valdes was an excellent psychologist in the New York City area. For decades she assisted men who experienced unwanted SSA. She developed a triadic-support system for her clients: 1) therapist, 2) client, and 3) spiritual director and/or mentor of the same gender. With the client's agreement, the therapist and spiritual director (or mentor) worked together to assist the patient.

17—Over the past four decades, therapy to assist those who experience unwanted SSA has had many different names, used by different therapists. Dr. Jospeh Nicolosi Sr. used the term "Reparative Therapy." He used the term "reparative" which was derived from the work of Dr. Elizabeth Moberly (*Homosexuality: A New Christian Ethic*, James Clarke & Co., 1983, revised 2006). She purported that the underlying motivation of those who experience SSA is a "reparative" drive, seeking to reclaim the unobtained love of the same-gender parents and/or same-gender peers. According to Moberly and Nicolosi, this "reparative" drive represents the soul's attempt to heal wounds and fulfill unmet love needs for secure attachment.

Dr. Joseph Nicolosi, Jr. (son of Dr. Nicolosi, Sr.) uses the term "Reintegrative Therapy" (https://www.reintegrativetherapy.com). Other therapists have used terms such as Sexual Orientation Change Efforts (SOCE), Gender Identity Change Efforts (GICE), Sexual Reorientation Therapy, and Gender Reaffirming Therapy.

Now with the ever-increasing pro-gay political landscape, I use the term Sexual Orientation Therapy. We, in this field of assisting those who experience unwanted SSA, must be mindful of the minefields that we must navigate in this ever-growing reverse-discriminatory world. Once we were the majority of therapists in the pre-1970s. Now we are on the outside and considered homophobic anti-gays, simply because we believe in what the science really says and the client's right of self-determination.

PART I: BLUEPRINT FOR HEALING

Simple Truths About Same-Sex Attraction (SSA)

1. There is no compelling evidence that anyone is determined from birth to experience SSA.

There is no conclusive scientific data that proves there is a simple genetic, biologic or hormonal cause for SSA. Scientific research indicates that although biological and/or genetic factors may play a part, homosexual desires stem from a complex interaction of psychological, environmental, and temperamental influences.

2. No one simply chooses to have SSA.

These desires are very often the result of unresolved childhood wounds and legitimate unmet love needs. It is a bio-psycho-social phenomenon arising from many factors. Therefore, no one simply chooses to experience SSA. The decision whether or not to act upon these desires is clearly a choice.

3. People can be hopeful in their choice to change from SSA to OSA.

Research demonstrates that change *is* possible. With strong motivation, effective treatment, and proper support, some people can and do change. The path to healing is fourfold:

1) Understand the root causes of SSA.
2) Gain support from others.
3) Heal the wounds that created the desires in the first place.
4) Fulfill unmet love needs in healthy, healing, nonsexual relationships with those of the same gender.

The field of Neuroplasticity, through numerous scientific studies, has shown that both the brain and behavior can change. "Neuroplasticity is the brain's capacity to continue growing and evolving in response to life experiences. Plasticity is the capacity to be shaped, molded, or altered; neuroplasticity, then, is the ability for the brain to adapt or change over time, by creating new neurons and building new networks" (https://www.psychologytoday.com/us/basics/neuroplasticity). Read Dr. Norman Doidge's groundbreaking book, *The Brain that Changes Itself* (New York: Penguin Life, 2007).

Since the 1990s, we have heard only one hand clapping in media messaging, "People are born gay." But in fact, what the real science says is "No one is essentially born with SSA."

The American Psychological Association, a strictly gay-affirming organization, finally admitted:

"Although much research has examined the possible genetic, hormonal, developmental, social, and cultural influences on sexual orientation, no findings have emerged that permit scientists to conclude that sexual orientation is determined by any particular factor or factors."

American Psychological Association, 2008
http://www.apa.org/topics/sorientation.html

And according to the American College of Pediatricians:

- Homosexuality is not a genetically determined, unchangeable trait.
- Homosexual attraction is determined by a combination of familial, environmental, social and biological influences. Inheritance predisposing personality traits may play a role for some. Consequently, homosexual attraction is changeable.
- The homosexual lifestyle, especially for males, carries grave health risks.
- Sexual reorientation therapy has proven effective for those with unwanted homosexual attractions.

www.FactsAboutYouth.com

Dr. Francis Collins, M.D., Ph.D., is the Director of the National Institutes of Health, the U.S.A. government's research organization. In his book, *The Language of God: A Scientist Presents Evidence for Belief* (New York: Free Press, 2006, page 260), Dr. Collins states:

"An area of particularly strong public interest is the genetic basis of homosexuality. Evidence from twin studies does in fact support the conclusion that heritable factors play a role in male homosexuality. However, the likelihood that the identical twin of a homosexual male will also be gay is about 20% (compared with 2-4 percent of males in the general population), indicating that sexual orientation is genetically influenced but not hardwired by DNA, and that whatever genes are involved represent predispositions, not predeterminations."

Dr. Neil and Briar Whitehead, in their book, with the ironic title, *My Genes Made Me Do It: A Scientific Look at Sexual Orientation,* debunks the studies that attempt to purport a genetic, biologic or hormonal basis for SSA (http://mygenes.co.nz/download.htm).

Sexuality and Gender: Findings from the Biological, Psychological, and Social Sciences was published in The New Atlantis by Lawrence S. Mayer, Ph.D. and Paul McHugh, M.D., in 2016 (www.thenewatlantis.com). This study, conducted by world-renowned Johns Hopkins University scientists, is a meta-analysis of data from over 200 peer-reviewed studies regarding "sexual orientation" and "gender identity." It is the most objective, exhaustive and comprehensive study on the topic to date. Highlights of the study:

PART I: BLUEPRINT FOR HEALING

- The understanding of sexual orientation as an innate, biologically fixed property of human beings—the idea that people are "born that way"—is not supported by scientific evidence (page 7 and Part One: Sexual Orientation).
- Sexual orientation in adolescents is fluid over the life course for some people, with one study estimating that as many as 80 percent of male adolescents who report same-sex attractions no longer do so as adults (page 7 and Part One).
- Compared to heterosexuals, non-heterosexuals are about two to three times as likely to have experienced childhood sexual abuse (page 7 and Part One).
- Compared to the general population, non-heterosexual sub-populations are at an elevated risk for a variety of adverse health and mental health outcomes (page 8 and Part Two: Sexuality, Mental Health Outcomes, and Social Stress).
- Members of the non-heterosexual population are estimated to have about 1.5 times higher risk of experiencing anxiety disorders than members of the heterosexual population, as well as roughly double the risk of depression, 1.5 times the risk of substance abuse, and nearly 2.5 times the risk of suicide (page 8 and Part Two).
- The hypothesis that gender identity is an innate, fixed property of human beings that is

independent of biological sex—that a person might be "a man trapped in a woman's body" or "a woman trapped in a man's body"—is not supported by scientific evidence (page 8 and Part Three: Gender Identity).

- Members of the transgender population are also at higher risk of a variety of mental health problems compared to members of the non-transgender population. Especially alarmingly, the rate of lifetime suicide attempts across all ages of transgender individuals is estimated at 41%, compared to under 5% in the overall U.S. population (page 8 and Part Two).
- Studies comparing the brain structures of transgender and non-transgender individuals ... do not provide any evidence for a neurobiological basis for cross-gender identification (page 8 and Part Three: Gender Identity).
- Compared to the general population, adults who have undergone sex-reassignment surgery continue to have a higher risk of experiencing poor mental health outcomes. One study found that, compared to controls, sex-reassigned individuals were about five times more likely to attempt suicide and about 19 times more likely to die by suicide (page 9 and Part Three).
- Only a minority of children who experience cross-gender identification will continue to do

so in adolescence or adulthood (page 9 and Part Three).
- There is no evidence that all children who express gender-atypical thoughts or behavior should be encouraged to become transgender (page 9 and Part Three).

There is (Still) No Gay Gene, 2019

A study was reported in the journal *Science* in 2019. The researchers were from Harvard and MIT. The subjects were 470,000 people who identified as gay. They gave permission for their DNA to be tested. This study was 100 times larger than any group previously studied. Their conclusion was that there is no way to look at someone's DNA and predict whether they are gay or straight:
- https://www.harvardmagazine.com/2019/08/there-s-still-no-gay-gene#:~:text=There%20is%20no%20one%20genecomplex%2C%20and%20anything%20but%20deterministic%20and%20
- https://www.nature.com/articles/d41586-%20019-02585-6

Meaning Behind Same-Sex Attraction (SSA)

Homosexuality is a symptom of:

- Unhealed wounds of the past (ten potential causes)
- Unmet needs for love
- Reparative drive to fulfill homo-emotional and/or homo-social love needs

Homosexuality is essentially an emotionally-based condition:

- Need for same-gender parent's/same-gender peers' love
- Need for gender indentification
- Fear of intimacy with members of the opposite sex

SSA represents a lack of gender indentity, caused by:

- Detachment from same-gender parent
- Detachment from same-gender peers
- Detachment from one's body
- Detachment from one's own gender

© Richard Cohen, M.A., 2023

As you will soon discover, there are many contributing factors that lead a boy or girl to develop homosexual feelings. Many professional therapists, myself included, have observed that most often SSA men and women are highly sensitive or hypersensitive individuals. Therefore, they experience events and relationships more deeply than other children. This temperament of hypersensitivity often leads these boys and girls to *perceive* rejection from their parents, peers, family members and/or friends. This perception becomes their reality: "I don't fit in. I'm different. I don't belong." These are often the core beliefs of children and adolescents who experience SSA.

If you are a parent of an SSA child, please do not blame yourself. This is not a blame game. My sole purpose in identifying what may have occurred is to achieve healing and reconciliation. Knowledge is power. Understanding the deeper meaning behind homosexual feelings is instrumental to bring about lasting change.

1. Homosexuality is a symptom of:

- Unhealed wounds of the past (see ten potential causes)
- Unmet needs for love
- Reparative drive to fulfill homo-emotional and/or homo-social love needs

Homosexual feelings, thoughts and desires are symptoms of underlying issues. They represent (1) a defensive response to conflicts in the present, a way to medicate pain, (2) unresolved childhood trauma, emotions and wounds that never healed, and (3) a *reparative drive* to fulfill homo-emotional love needs (bonding with same-gender parent, i.e., father-son, mother-daughter) and/or homo-social love needs (bonding with same-gender peers, i.e., guys with guys, girls with girls).

By "reparative drive" we mean that the individual who experiences SSA is seeking to obtain the love he or she did not experience in early childhood and adolescence, and is doing so by trying to connect with someone of the same gender. I need to stress that this reparative drive is most often completely unconscious. Dr. Elizabeth Moberly coined and Dr. Jospeh Nicolosi Sr. further developed the concept of a homo-emotional love need.

> "It is here suggested that it is precisely this reparative urge that is involved in the homosexual impulse, that is, that this impulse is essentially motivated by the need to make good earlier deficits in the parent-child relationship. This persisting need for love from the same sex stems from, and is to be correlated with, the earlier unmet need for love from the parent of the same sex, or rather, the inability to receive such love, whether or not it was offered. This defensive detachment and its corresponding drive for renewed attachment imply that the homosexual condition is one of same-sex ambivalence" Elizabeth R. Moberly, *Homosexuality: A New Christian Ethic* (Cambridge, UK: Lutterworth Press, revised edition 2006), 6.

2. Homosexuality is essentially an emotionally based condition:

- Need for same-gender parent's / same-gender peers' love
- Need for gender identification
- Fear of intimacy with members of the opposite sex

We gain our sense of gender identity—masculinity for a man, and femininity for a woman—through successful bonding with our same-gender parent and then same-gender relatives and peers. Most case histories of those who experience SSA demonstrate that homosexual feelings originate in early childhood and preadolescence.

From the ages of one or one-and-a-half to three, the child begins to crawl, walk and then talk. This stage of development is known as a time of separation and individuation. The child begins to realize that he/she is different from mom, that he/she is an individual, separate and unique from mother. This time is also known as either the terrible or terrific twos, and the operative word is, "No." "No" essentially means that "I am not you, I am me, and I'm different from you." *However, the boy has an extra developmental task here.* He comes to realize that his genitals are different from his mother's. Who does he look like, who does he resemble?

The boy must then gender identify with his father, his role model of masculinity. If the father is absent, abusive or distant, another male mentor may help stand in the gap for the son. If there is no strong male presence in the toddler's life, he may continue to gender identify with his mother, internalizing her sense of femininity. This is one reason why many men who experience SSA may say, "From the time I was a child, I experienced homosexual feelings." They never successfully individuated from their mothers and gender identified with their fathers. On the other hand, the daughter, even though she is separating and individuating from her mother, will continue to gender identify with mom as her primary role model of femininity. She individuates while continuing to emulate her mother's behaviors. In the case of a potential SSA daughter, she may have been fearful of or detested her mother, and therefore didn't successfully internalize her own sense of femaleness (see other causes listed below).

> "Just when he was developing his sense of masculinity and was especially receptive to the father's influence, the prehomosexual boy experienced a hurt or disappointment in his relationship with his father. To protect himself against future hurt, the boy developed a defensive posture characterized by emotional distancing. Not only does he fail to identify with father, but because of this hurt, he rejects father and the masculinity he represents" Joseph Nicolosi Sr., *Reparative Therapy of Male Homosexuality: A New Clinical Approach*

PART I: BLUEPRINT FOR HEALING

(Northvale, NJ: Jason Aronson, Inc., 1991, Liberal Mind Publishers, updated edition, 2020), 105.

Same-sex attraction often represents a search for healthy parenting—a man seeking paternal love in the arms of another man, and a woman seeking maternal love in the arms of another woman (of course, this drive is most often unconscious). It may also represent a need for bonding with same-gender peers because these men and women never experienced successful bonding with those of the same gender in their preadolescent and/or adolescent years of development. Then, during puberty, those normal needs for bonding, with the same-gender parent and/or same-gender peers, became sexualized and/or eroticized. At this point the world tends to say to such a person, "You're born gay," or "You're born lesbian." This is a false label.

Labeling people with words like gay, lesbian, bisexual, or transgender is not only false, it also is done without a proper understanding of the situation. We are born as a man or a woman, as a son or a daughter. Those who experience SSA are merely stuck in early stages of psychosexual development. When they resolve past issues and fulfill unmet love needs in healthy, nonsexual, same-gender relationships, they will naturally develop opposite-sex desires. We are all heterosexually designed (men and women fit together beautifully and perfectly, biologically two men or two women simply do not).

If a man seeks to join sexually with another man, it means there is something lacking within him. He does not experience the fullness of his own masculinity. By joining with a man, he hopes to complete this lost part of himself. The same holds true for the woman seeking to join sexually with another woman. These yearnings represent the deep need of a child within—a need to experience love and secure bonding with someone of the same gender, to restore this lack of love. However, sexual relations will never satiate that need for love because this need is that of a child, and children do not want or need sex.

In many cases men who experience SSA have been over-attached to their mothers and detached from their fathers and the masculinity they represented. As a result of closeness to his mom and detachment from his dad, the son becomes internally more feminine in nature (research shows that about 85% of adult men who experience SSA had a close-binding intimate relationship with their mothers). In adulthood, this may block his ability to have a successful heterosexual relationship with another woman, because of this over-attachment and identification with the feminine (remember, opposites attract). The same may hold true for the daughter who is over-attached to her father and disconnected and dis-identified with her mother. She internalizes her dad's masculinity and rejects her mother's femininity. She may spend the rest of her life looking for that lost love and sense of connection with the feminine in the arms of other women.

> "In one popular scenario of the homosexual male, he is the son of an unhappily married woman whose unhealthy, engulfing relationship with him may border on the incestuous. Though he becomes symbolically 'mother's little love,' she may stifle the boy's embryonic masculinity lest the relationship become overtly incestuous. However far it goes, he has feelings of guilt. Later, as an adult, he associates this guilt with all women because they remind him of the 'forbidden mother,' and therefore must not be touched. Many male homosexuals confess to strong attachments to their mothers, beginning from earliest childhood when their fathers were either absent, weak, withdrawn, or extremely harsh. Through this attachment, they 'identify' with women and seek the same sexual outlets as women" Robert Kronemeyer, *Overcoming Homosexuality* (New York City: NY, Macmillan Publishing Co., Inc., 1980), 60-61.

Many women who experience SSA might have also been sexually, physically, emotionally and/or mentally abused by men, and/or are hypersensitive. Not wanting to re-experience abuse with men, many turn to other women for affection, comfort and love. It is interesting to note that there is a higher percentage of domestic violence among lesbian couples than there is in the heterosexual population. Why? Underneath the exterior of these women are hurt little girls who were violated, and who take out their aggression and unresolved pain on each other.

The father of Cathy, an SSA woman, had had many affairs. He was loud, angry, judgmental and strict. Cathy developed anxiety around her dad as well as other men, and therefore turned to women for her affectional needs, seeking safety in their arms. Another SSA woman, Barbara, had parents who were always busy. She felt invisible to them. She clung to her brothers for attention and affection, even though they mistreated and abused her. Barbara feared revealing her heart to anyone and longed for a woman to just hold her in her arms.

Psychotherapist Janelle Hallman, in her landmark book, *The Heart of Female Same-Sex Attraction* (Westmont, IL: InterVarsity Press, 2008), mentions four types of profiles for women who experience SSA. "They are primarily descriptive in nature and should *not* be rigidly construed: indeed, many women *may* identify with one profile over another, but will most likely see parts of themselves in each of the other profiles as well" Hallman, 159.

- **"Profile 1: Empty, Depressed, Withdrawn and Isolated**. These women often have profound developmental deficits arising out of perceived and actual emotional absence or neglect. Their basic physical needs were met, but they nevertheless internalized the message that their existence was an inconvenience and a nuisance. Their lives are severely empty and lonely. They have a few friends, but the friendships lack mutuality. They feel more attached to objects or animals than to people. They are uncomfortable in their own skin and know that they are not 'normal,' at least in social settings. They may show marked inability to follow standard social cueing or comprehend—let alone articulate—inner emotional or psychological dynamics. They are often overweight and tend to be nondescript in appearance" Hallman, 160.

- **"Profile 2: Tough, Angry, Sarcastic and Barricaded**. These women often have the worst histories of trauma and abuse, frequently involving severe physical or emotional abandonment, although this is not always the case. For some, the environments in which they were raised were not hostile, but the women nevertheless sensed and were negatively affected by the underlying relational dysfunctions within the family system. Both groups of women carry a deep belief that the world is not safe. Those in this profile have relied on toughness (rather than the deadness found among profile 1 women) to protect their tender hearts. They are often overwhelmingly disillusioned to discover that their method of survival—severe defensiveness—actually starves them of intimacy. Unlike those associated with profile 1, they can feel their inner agony and therefore aggressively and continuously 'cut off' all vulnerabilities. They work hard but are demanding; they are impatient but also deeply committed. If they decide that you are safe, they will do anything in the world for you. They have an endless ability to care for and take care of others, all the while denying their own needs" Hallman, 165.

- **"Profile 3: Energetic, Caretaking, Drama-Oriented, and never 'Home.'** Even though these women are less likely to have typical trauma or neglect in their background as compared to women associated with profiles 1 and 2, they still suffer from severe, subtle and negative relational dynamics such as familial enmeshment or rigid gender roles within their families of origin. Due to their attuned sensitivities and perhaps their deeper relational needs, they felt that they were neither acknowledged nor affirmed as special, particularly as a girl. Although they felt close and loved, they also felt obligated to support or take care of other family members, including Mom and Dad. Nevertheless, their basic needs were usually met, and they experience the greatest level of stability among the four profiles. They are active, often athletic and typically overachieving women" Hallman, 170.

- **"Profile 4: Pragmatic, Perfectionistic, Distant and Smugly Self-Assured**. Women with this profile have various backgrounds but typically compensate for their losses and defend against their pain by avoiding all vulnerability and identifying with their ability to pursue excellence and success. They are often the movers and shakers within their field of expertise and find their kudos through achievement. They are very intelligent and extremely gifted. But because they are often so accomplished, they are also arrogant and contemptuous of others (especially men). They may unconsciously use others to serve their own purpose or meet their own needs" Hallman, 176.

Dr. Hallman concludes by appealing to her reader: *Please do not reduce an SSA woman to one profile. There is more to her than a simple description. The only useful purpose of these categories is to learn how to assist each woman in her healing process.* I hope you will read her book for a more comprehensive understanding of female SSA.

3. SSA represents a lack of gender identity, caused by:

- Detachment from same-gender parent
- Detachment from same-gender peers
- Detachment from one's body
- Detachment from one's own gender

SSA often represents detachment between the individual and his or her same-gender parent and/or same-gender peers. Because a boy did not successfully or sufficiently bond with his dad and/or other male relatives and peers, he then rejects his own gender identity, not wanting to act or be like his father and/or other boys. After this occurs and puberty sets in, his emotional needs for bonding become sexualized. This is the construction of SSA and perhaps a gay identity—little boys and girls in adolescent or adult bodies looking for bonding through sexual relationships. Sexual behavior cannot and will not resolve their deeper needs.

PART I: BLUEPRINT FOR HEALING

Ten Potential Causes of SSA

Because I have come out of homosexuality and have helped others do the same, I understand this condition from the inside out. Over the past five decades, I have read countless studies and books on the etiology and treatment of ego dystonic homosexuality. Once again, SSA is not about SSA or sex. There is no such thing as a homosexual (noun). There are only people who experience same-sex attraction (adjective) and/or practice homosexual behaviors.

The following is a list of ten potential causes that may lead an individual to experience SSA (see the chart below). A combination of innate temperament, familial relationships and environmental factors lead an individual to experience SSA—never a single factor alone. Parents do not instill SSA in their children. It is the child's perception of their parenting combined with his/her innate temperament, e.g. hypersensitivity, which makes the difference. You may read stories of transformation in *Being Gay* and watch, read or listen to wonderful stories of change at http://www.voicesofchange.net.

1. Heredity

- Unresolved family issues
- Misperceptions
- Tendency to feel rejected

A THERAPIST'S GUIDE

Potential Variables Creating Same-Sex Attraction

Heredity	Temperament	Hetero-Emotional Wounds	Homo-Emotional Wounds	Sibling Wounds/ Family Dynamics	Body Image Wounds	Sexual Abuse	Social or Peer Wounds	Cultural Wounds	Others Factors
Generational Blessings and curses	Hypersensitive	Over-attachment to opposite-sex parent	Lack of attachment to same-sex parent	Abuse: mental, emotional, physical, and/or sexual	Late bloomer	Premature sexualization	Name-calling	Internet porn	Divorce
Unresolved family issues	High Maintenance	Abuse: mental, emotional, physical, and/or sexual	Abuse: mental, emotional, physical, and/or sexual	Don't fit in	Physical disabilities	Homosexual imprinting	Put-downs	Media/Entertainment Industry promoting sex	Death
Men resenting women, women resenting men	Artistic Nature	Parentified child: role reversal between parent and child	Parentified child: role reversal between parent and child	Don't belong	Shorter / Taller	Learned/ reinforced behavior	Teacher's pet	Sexualizing legitimate needs for love	Suicide
Addictions: substances, sex, gambling	Gender non-conforming behaviors	Born the wrong sex	Born the wrong sex	Different from others	Heavier / Thinner	Sex used as a substitute for love	Goody-goody		Addictions: alcohol, drugs, sex, gambling, etc.
Medical/Mental health issues	Male more feminine	Imitation of behavior		Bullying/ verbal abuse	Skin color issues		Nerd		Intra-uterine experience: insecure attachment
Financial problems	Female more masculine				Lack of eye-hand coordination		Non-athletic		Adoption
Predilection for rejection							Lack of gender identification and/or gender non-conforming behaviors		War/genocide
Racial, religious, ethnic prejudice									Religion: toxic beliefs

The severity of wounding in each category will have a direct impact on the amount of time and effort it will take to heal.

Richard Cohen, M.A. © 2023

PART I: BLUEPRINT FOR HEALING

"It is assumed [by Intergenerational and Transgenerational Family Systems Theory] that relational patterns are learned and passed down across the generations and that current individual and family behavior is a result of these patterns" James Bray and Donald Williamson, "Assessment of Intergenerational Family Relationships," *Family of Origin Therapy*, (Rockville, MD: Aspen Publishers, 1987), 31.

In family systems therapy, it is well known and accepted that unresolved issues and dysfunctional behaviors of preceding generations are passed down to subsequent family members. At the core of an individual who experiences SSA is a sense of not belonging, not fitting in, and feeling different from others. These thoughts and feelings may be passed down from family members, over many generations, depending upon their circumstances in life, culture, religion, race and/or ethnicity.

"Recent developments in the fields of cellular biology, neuroscience, epigenetics, and developmental psychology underscore the importance of exploring at least three generations of family history in order to understand the mechanism behind patterns of trauma and suffering that repeat" Mark Wolynn, *It Didn't Start with You: How Inherited Family Trauma Shapes Who We*

Are and How to End the Cycle (New York: Penguin Books, 2017), 17.

What I and other sexual orientation therapists have observed is that men and women who experience SSA are highly susceptible to rejection, or perceived rejection, existing for any number of reasons which may stem from unresolved generational issues. Of course, this does not by itself cause same-sex attraction in boys or girls; it is just one contributing factor among many.

At the same time, the emerging field of epigenetics (literally, "on" or "above" our genes), has demonstrated that while we inherit a hard-wired and fixed genome from our parents at birth (and pass ours on to our children in the same way), the genes that comprise our DNA sequence are themselves dynamic and active. They are turned on or off by signals from our environment, including our emotions and life experiences. Epigenetic gene expression suggests that we may inherit from our forebears and pass on to our descendants such fluid and flexible experiences as trauma, capacity for self-regulation (or lack thereof), and predispositions to behavioral and mental health challenges.

2. Temperament

- Hypersensitive
- Artistic nature

- Gender nonconforming behaviors: male more feminine, female more masculine

As I have observed in my clinical practice, many or most men and women who experience SSA were hypersensitive from childhood. This innate temperament led them to react more deeply to the behaviors of their parents, relatives and peers. Often attuned to the emotions of their parents, these children would frequently modify their behaviors to avoid conflict. At other times they became pleasers or caretakers. Because of their hypersensitive nature, they may have acted more passively and therefore were unable to assert themselves in interpersonal relationships. Of course, not all hypersensitive children will develop SSA. It is, again, just one contributing factor.

If the hypersensitive child had an artistic nature, and the parents, relatives or peers were non-supportive of this gift, she or he may have experienced further rejection. The sensitive and gifted child, in an insensitive and unsupportive environment, experiences undue stress and anxiety.

A further group of young children, who exhibit what we call "gender non-conforming behaviors," that is, the little boy who acts more effeminate and the little girl who acts more masculine, are particularly at risk for being either ostracized by family members and/or peers. On the other hand, these days, they are encouraged to act upon those tendencies (the new transgender phenomenon). However, these character traits or behavioral phenotypes—the more effeminate boy and the more masculine girl—in certain environments may be expressed with the purpose of invoking a reparative or healing drive. Let me explain. Instead of thinking, "Oh, he was meant to be a girl," or "She was meant to be a boy," we may be viewing an opportunity, through the birth of this child, to heal generational wounds of detachment between either fathers and sons or mothers and daughters.

I have worked with many parents of young children who exhibit gender non-conforming behaviors. I first ask about the relationships between the parents and all their children. Then I seek to understand at least three generations in their family system (both sides with their parents and grandparents). Patterns emerge which help to explain the birth and behavior of the more effeminate-acting boy, or masculine-acting female. It then becomes clearer how to coach the parents in their bonding relationship with this child.

Scientific studies have shown when bonding and healthy attachment is achieved between this gender non-conforming child and his or her same-gender parent, then secure gender identity will ensue (Zucker, K. J. *Children and adolescents with gender dysphoria*. In Y. M. Binik and K. S. K. Hall (Eds.), Principles and practices of sex therapy (Sixth ed.). New York: Guilford Press, 2020). See Dr. Zucker's website for more information: https://www.kenzuckerphd.com.

Therefore, with this understanding, if the father would take the time to join with this effeminate boy, see life through his eyes and experiences, and create a strong alliance, eventually the boy may bond with his dad and internalize his father's sense of masculine identity. The same would hold true for the mother and her more masculine-acting daughter. I have successfully helped many parents, whose children exhibited gender non-conforming behaviors, to restore relationships and reorient their children to their original gender identity. More about this in the final section of the book.

As mentioned, Dr. Francis S. Collins, director of the National Institutes for Health and former director of the Human Genome Project, declares that homosexuality is "genetically influenced but not hardwired by DNA, and that whatever genes are involved represent predispositions, not predeterminations" (*The Language of God*, New York: Free Press, 2006), 260. With healthy intervention by parents and mentors, the child will experience a sense of his or her own gender identity.

3. Opposite-Gender (Hetero-Emotional) Parental Wounds

- Over attachment to opposite-gender parent (enmeshment)
- Imitation of opposite-gender behaviors

- Abuse: emotional, mental, verbal, physical and/or sexual

There has been much literature written about boys over-attached to their mothers and girls over-attached to their fathers. Again, this is not a blame game, but simply identifying what took place for the purpose of healing. Drs. Irving Bieber, Charles Socarides, Joseph Nicolosi, Gerard van den Aardweg, Robert Kronemeyer and many other psychologists and psychiatrists have observed that men who experience SSA have had an abnormally close mother-son attachment. They are inclined to internalize their mother's sense of femininity and become distant and detached from the masculinity represented by their fathers. Similarly, the daughter may be closer to her father and estranged from her mother, thereby internalizing her father's masculinity and rejecting her mother's femininity. In other cases, the daughter views the mother as weak and/or ineffective, and models her behavior after the more dominant and powerful parent, her father.

Another phenomenon might be the child perceiving that his or her parents wanted a child of the opposite gender. The son therefore acts like a girl, and the daughter acts like a boy in order to please their parents and win their approval and affection. As mentioned, many women who experience SSA have been abused by men, and not wanting to repeat these unhealthy bonding patterns, they seek their affectional needs from women.

PART I: BLUEPRINT FOR HEALING

4. Same-Gender (Homo-Emotional) Parental Wounds

- Detachment from same-gender parent
- Neglect: lack of intimacy
- Abuse: emotional, mental, verbal, physical and/or sexual

Forgive me for the repetition, however, it's imperative to understand this critical developmental task—lack of sufficient bonding between the son and his father and daughter and her mother is often at the core of anyone who experiences SSA (homo-emotional wound). Some of the experiences of detachment/neglect may be due to an angry, violent or scary parent, a physically or emotionally unavailable parent, etc. Additionally, because of the child's hypersensitive temperament, he or she may experience an even greater sense of rejection and therefore further detach from the same-gender parent. Also, a mismatch in character and temperament between father and son or mother and daughter often creates the sense of wounding in the heart of a pre-SSA child, e.g., an assertive, macho sports-oriented father and his artistic, hypersensitive son. For whatever reason(s), many children who experience SSA did not securely bond with the same-gender parent. Without the parent perceiving these cues, the daughter or son becomes susceptible to further rejection by same-gender peers. The stage is then set for the potential development of same-sex attraction and same-gender erotic feelings during or after puberty. Those desires represent a means to achieve bonding that never took place in the earliest years of child development.

5. Sibling Wounds / Family Dynamics

- Name calling
- Same-gender siblings/relatives' rejection
- Abuse: emotional, mental, verbal, sexual, and/or physical

Yet another variable that may contribute to the development of SSA is insufficient bonding with same-gender siblings and/or relatives of the same gender, e.g., boys with brothers and male relatives, or girls with sisters and female relatives. These hypersensitive children are often people-pleasers, trying to keep everyone happy at the expense of their own needs. Over the past 35 years as a psychotherapist, I have heard so many parents say, "My son was the perfect little boy." Well boys, generally by nature, are more assertive and mischievous, and not so sweet. Be careful of the "good little boys," encourage them to be themselves and not to please everyone else.

Some women who experience SSA had poor relationships with their sisters, and/or were mocked and teased by men in their family and social setting. This leaves a deep wound in their hearts, not fitting in with their same-gender peers and relatives, and/or feeling hurt by men. Some boys who experience SSA grew up in families of all girls and women, and some SSA girls grew up in families of all men. These factors may also contribute to gender confusion.

6. Body Image Wounds

- Late bloomer
- Shorter/taller—thinner/larger
- Physical disability

Late bloomer, early maturation, physical disabilities, shorter, taller, thinner, or larger—these are some characteristics that may result in body-image wounds for the pre-SSA boy or girl. A hypersensitive boy who experienced insufficient bonding with his father and over-attachment with his mother, now incurs more self-esteem issues by being different from other guys, e.g., too tall, too thin, too short, too large, not athletically inclined. The result may be a profound sense of gender inadequacy, feeling on the outside looking in. If they were late bloomers, they often felt different and alienated from their peers. The pre-SSA girl may experience similar thoughts and feelings based upon her perception of her body image and the opinions of her parents, relatives and/or peers.

7. Sexual Abuse

- Homosexual imprinting
- Learned and reinforced behaviors
- Substitute for affection and love

Sexual abuse may be another contributing factor to the development of same-sex attraction; however, it is never the sole cause. The pre-SSA child is more susceptible to sexual abuse because of his or her lack of attachment to the same-gender parent and/or same-gender peers. Sex then becomes a substitute or replacement for emotional and relational intimacy with others of the same gender. If the behavior is repeated over time, it may create a neurological basis for the further development of same-sex attraction in the male or female. Again, this is just another contributing factor and not a prerequisite to experience SSA. In my clinical practice, and the counseling practice of many colleagues, approximately 50% of our clients experienced some form of childhood sexual abuse.

There is usually a difference between SSA men and women when it comes to sexual abuse. Many boys who carry father and/or male peer wounds were easy targets for male sexual abuse, because they were longing for that connection and secure attachment with their dads and/or other boys. On the other hand, many girls develop SSA after being sexually abused by men. They may seek female affection to soothe their wounds and protect themselves from further abuse by men. Read more about this in Dr. Janelle Hallman's book.

8. Same-Gender (Homo-Social) Peer Wounds

- Name calling/put-downs
- Teacher's pet
- Non-athletic boy/more athletic girl

Both men and women who experience SSA often felt a tremendous sense of emotional wounding because of same-gender peer rejection—guys didn't fit in with other guys, and girls didn't fit in with other girls. Often, they were called names such as "sissy," "faggot," "queer," "pansy," "dyke," "tomboy." Many boys who experience SSA hung out with the girls, and many girls who experience SSA hung out with the guys. While boys who experience SSA may not have been athletically inclined and were teased and taunted by their male peers, some girls who experience SSA were more athletic, and if detached from their female peers, may have been ostracized as well. Then, during and/or after adolescence, those normal needs for same-gender peer bonding became sexualized. For a more in-depth explanation of how we sexualize our unmet attachment needs, read *Unwanted: How Sexual Brokenness Reveals Our Way to Healing*, Stringer, 2018.

Another source of wounding for the pre-SSA child is boys mocking girls ("You're so butch," "You're a dyke") and girls mocking boys ("You're such a faggot," "You're so sweet and girlie"). Not only do they receive put-downs from their same gender peers, but from their opposite gender peers as well.

9. Cultural Wounds

- Promotion of the homosexual myth—"born gay and cannot change"
- Cultural Abuse: media outlets, entertainment industry, educational system, online resources and politics, all affirming and promoting homosexuality
- Pornography

After a boy or girl experiences wounding or lack of attachment with their same-gender parent and/or same-gender peers, or incurs any of the other factors previously mentioned, then same-sex attractions may develop during or after adolescence leading to homo-erotic feelings and desires. The world then mistakenly says, "You're gay," "You're lesbian," etc. As we have learned, this is a false paradigm leading hurt children down the road to homosexuality under false pretenses. Also, with behaviors from performers in the music and entertainment industries, it is becoming trendy to experiment sexually and identify as LGBTQ+, non-binary, etc.

Many kids are being raised in single-parent families, often lacking the attention and affection of the same-gender parent. This leaves him or her more vulnerable to being enrolled into the false LGBTQ+ paradigm, whereby their normal needs for bonding will become eroticized with members of the same gender. The media outlets, educational system and entertainment industry, driven by the homosexual myth, have created false identities:

LGBTQ+. But there is no such thing as a "gay." There are only hurt children looking for love in ways that will not fulfill their deepest needs.

The Gay Rights Movement has indoctrinated people into believing the innate, immutable myth ("born gay and cannot change"). If boys or girls experience SSA in adolescence, we immediately label them as gay or lesbian, rather than understand there are specific causes that led him or her to experience SSA. *No one is essentially born this way.* There are always reasons why anyone develops homosexual feelings. (Some kids experiment sexually with same-gender friends at the onset of adolescence, but this does not make them gay or SSA.)

10. Other Factors

- Divorce
- Death
- Adoption
- Religion
- Spiritual factors

There are any number of other potentially traumatic experiences that may contribute towards the development of SSA and low self-worth in a hypersensitive boy or girl. If the parents divorce, the people-pleasing child may blame himself or herself. If a parent dies, the child may perceive it as personal rejection and abandonment. When a struggling child hears "hell and damnation" or homosexuality is an "abomination" from the pulpit of his or her place of worship, further feelings of guilt and shame burden this hypersensitive youth.

If the child was adopted, she or he may feel rejected by their birth parents and never securely attach to their adopted parents (read Greg Louganis's profile in *Understanding Our LGBTQ+ Loved Ones*). This sense of rejection may reside deep in the unconscious, creating a pattern of insecurity.

> Note: Many people with a strong faith background believe there might be spiritual influences that drive homosexual feelings in boys or girls and men or women. Even if there is validity to this, it is imperative to realize that when the other potential causes are addressed, healing occurs and change ensues. By strictly viewing SSA as a "spiritual problem," one will not fully heal and fulfill his or her innate heterosexual potential. As Christian psychotherapist Jan Frank stated, "You cannot heal a spirit, or deliver a wound."

A combination of any of these ten factors may lead an individual to experience SSA: (1) Heredity, (2) Temperament, (3) Hetero-emotional wounds, (4) Homo-emotional wounds, (5) Sibling wounds and family dynamics, (6) Body-image wounds, (7) Sexual abuse, (8) Social and peer wounds, (9) Cultural wounds, and (10)

Other factors. *The severity of wounding in each category will have a direct impact upon the amount of time and effort it will take to heal.* Please read *Being Gay: Nature, Nurture or Both?* for a more detailed explanation, with numerous references to scientific studies about the ten potential causes of SSA.

Let me be perfectly clear: I am not saying that people who decide to live a homosexual life are wrong. I respect all members of the LGBTQ+ (Lesbian, Gay, Bisexual, Transgender, Queer/Questioning +) community and the path that they have chosen. For me, I chose a different path, the "road less traveled," and, as Robert Frost has written, "that has made all the difference." What I wish to convey is that people are not essentially born with SSA, no one simply chooses to experience SSA, and that change *is* possible for those who pursue this option. The fact that there are underlying causes of homosexual feelings and there exists the potential for change is *not* widely publicized. There has existed for decades a heavily financed media mechanism which has suppressed this option for change.

A THERAPIST'S GUIDE

Seven Stages of "Coming Out"

I would like to share with you what I have discovered—seven stages leading to "coming out" as LGBTQ+. The following descriptions come from my book *Gay Children, Straight Parents* (Bowie, MD: PATH Press, 2016), 18-24:

Stage 1 – Causes of SSA
Stage 2 – Same-sex attractions begin
Stage 3 – Conflict over SSA
Stage 4 – Need for belonging
Stage 5 – Indoctrination
Stage 6 – Identity acceptance as gay, lesbian, bisexual, transgender, non-binary, etc.
Stage 7 – "Coming out" process

Stage 1: Causes of SSA. I just mentioned the many contributing factors that result in homosexual desires such as disrupted attachment between father and son or mother and daughter (this may be the child's perception, not the parent's failure), over-attachment to the opposite-gender parent, hypersensitivity, lack of bonding with same-gender peers, sibling wounds, cultural wounds, name-calling, sexual abuse and/or body image wounds. Again, it is never one thing alone that causes SSA, but a combination of variables.

Stage 2: Same-sex attractions begin. SSA begins at various stages and ages for different people depending on several factors: the child's temperament, physiology and perceptions; family history at particular times; and social or cultural events. Most often, the eroticization of another person of the same gender begins around ten to thirteen years of age, near the onset of puberty. In some cases, the desires may occur sooner if a child has undergone sexual abuse or some other significant trauma (e.g. early exposure to sex, divorce or death of a parent, introduction to online porn from a young age). For some, homosexual desires may emerge later on, in the late teens or early twenties, or in other cases during a mid-life crisis. More and more married men and women are "coming out" and often times disclosing their long battle with SSA. Such individuals may have repressed their same-sex attractions for many years, hoping and praying they would disappear.

Stage 3: Conflict over SSA. The young struggler may ask himself/herself, "Why do I have these feelings? What would others think about me if they knew I had homosexual desires?" A child may wonder, "Is it a sin to feel this way? Does God still love me?" Most often, these boys and girls experience tremendous feelings of guilt, shame, confusion and loneliness. These emotions are exacerbated when the young person is unable or unwilling to talk freely with family and friends. He or she may be involved in a strong religious community and may hesitate to disclose about his or her SSA for fear of being rejected and judged.

Kids today easily find "answers" outside their immediate circle of loved ones and spiritual community. They access pro-homosexual information on the Internet or attend a Gay Straight Alliance (GSA) meeting in middle or high school, or an LGBTQ+ club in college. The new addition to the LGBTQ+ nomenclature is "Q" meaning "Queer" or "Questioning" youth, so that people who have a fleeting attraction for someone of the same gender may be led to believe that they are gay, bisexual or queer.

As mentioned, some young children experiment with members of their own sex while entering adolescence. Others have had sexual encounters while intoxicated, and others while attending boarding school. This does not make these young people same-sex attracted or gay. This is situational behavior and the majority of these individuals move on to develop strictly heterosexual feelings and desires.

Stage 4: Need for belonging. The struggle continues: "I don't fit in. I don't belong. I'm not like the other kids." During puberty, what were once emotional desires for bonding with the same-gender parent and/or same-gender peers, now become sexually inflamed yearnings. The emotional need for nonsexual intimacy with the same-gender parent and/or same-gender peers suddenly becomes eroticized. However intense the desire may feel, it is important to remember that the basis for all SSA is unhealed wounds of the past and unmet love needs.

Stage 5: Indoctrination. As we see in the world today, any young person who experiences even a minimum amount of same-sex attraction is told, "You were born gay. You cannot change. Efforts to change are harmful." These youths have to work very hard to accept themselves as gay, lesbian, bisexual or queer. This process generates conflicting thoughts and feelings. I believe that those who experience SSA initially know, in their conscience, that homosexual behavior is out of sync with natural law. Nonetheless, they are inundated with the idea that SSA is genetically, biologically or hormonally determined—they're born that way, therefore, they cannot change.

The "born gay" myth is much like the old folktale *The Emperor's New Clothes*. In this story, an emperor is fooled into believing skilled craftsmen are creating beautiful clothes for him. In fact, two charlatans have created nothing. Going along with the hoax, the emperor parades through the city streets wearing nothing but his underwear. Not wanting to appear foolish, all his subjects exclaim, "What a wonderful set of new clothes!" Then a child stands up and says, "The emperor is naked!" At that moment the emperor realizes he has been duped. "We should all be like this child and speak the truth," he proclaims. So it is today. Most of us have been deceived, even though we instinctively know that humans are heterosexually designed.

Stage 6: Identity acceptance as gay, lesbian, bisexual, transgender or queer/questioning. At this juncture, strugglers come to terms with their SSA and adopt a gay, lesbian, bisexual, transgender, queer or non-binary identity. They have anesthetized their conscience through social indoctrination and finally self-acceptance. Hearing the homosexual myth repeated often enough, with little or no debate, establishes it as "fact." At this stage, you and the rest of the "homophobic" society may be perceived as the enemy. (A phobia is an irrational fear of something, not a principled disagreement. Gay activists have purposely misused this term.) "You don't understand. You don't know what it's like to be gay, and what its like to be on the outside looking in." The us-versus-them mentality is reinforced.

Stage 7: "Coming out" process. Often parents are the last to know about a child's SSA, not because they are the least important, but because they are the most important. Gender-confused young people are especially hypersensitive and fearful of rejection, so they first "come out" to their friends, teachers or relatives who seem to be safer. They are developing a support system fearing that mom and/or dad may reject them. Finally, he may share with his parents, "Please accept me for who I am. I'm your gay son. God made me this way!" Or she may angrily exclaim, "If you refuse to accept me just the way I am, you're homophobic and unloving." The truth is, they are afraid to lose their parents' love, and naturally parents are afraid of losing their child's love.

PART I: BLUEPRINT FOR HEALING

How to Assist Those Who Experience Unwanted SSA

Through my own journey of healing, and through my clinical practice since 1989, I have developed a four-stage model of recovery. It has proved successful for those who experience unwanted same-sex attraction, whether they have been sexually active or not. The same protocol applies to both populations. Additionally, heterosexual marriage is never the solution for anyone who experiences SSA, because a woman can never meet the homo-emotional/homo-social needs of a man, and a man can never meet the homo-emotional/homo-social needs of a woman. In the process of recovery, first a man must heal with other men, and a woman must heal with other women.

> "Attempted heterosexual relationships, or social contact, with the opposite sex, are not the solution to homosexuality, since increased opposite-sex contact can do nothing to fulfill same-sex deficits" Elizabeth R. Moberly, *Homosexuality: A New Christian Ethic* (Cambridge, UK: Lutterworth Press, revised edition 2006), 18.

Over the years, I basically had four types of clients:
1) Young people confused about their sexuality and/or gender identity.
2) Married men or women (in heterosexual marriages) who wish to resolve their unwanted SSA.

3) Those who lived a gay/lesbian life, never found the right person(s), and wish to explore the possibility of change.
4) Religiously motivated men and women who sought to resolve their unwanted SSA.

Of course, the first three types may also be motivated to resolve unwanted SSA because of their spiritual beliefs.

Before I sought help, some of my well-intentioned friends told me, "Richard, just find the right woman and she'll straighten you out," or "Just pray hard enough, and God will take those desires away. If not, then you're doing something wrong." Well, I wish it would have been that simple, but it was not. I prayed and prayed for God to take away my SSA, but He did not. I married, hoping it would straighten me out, but my same-sex desires only intensified. I came to understand that I had been praying the wrong prayer for over twenty years. What I needed to pray was: "God, please reveal to me the meaning behind my same-sex desires." Later, I understood that God could have but would not take away my SSA, because it was connected to the hurts in my heart that required healing, and legitimate needs for love that required fulfillment in healthy non-sexual relationships with heterosexual mentors and friends.

I have divided the process of healing into four stages:

PART I: BLUEPRINT FOR HEALING

Four Stages of Resolving Unwanted Same-Sex Attraction (SSA)

Stage One: Transitioning (Behavioral Therapy)

- Cutting off from sexual behaviors: playgrounds, playmates, playthings
- Developing a Support Network
- Building self-worth and experiencing value in relationship with God

Stage Two: Grounding (Cognitive Therapy)

- Continuing with the Support Network
- Continuing to build self-worth and experience value in relationship with God
- Building skills: assertiveness training, communication skills, problem-solving techniques
- Beginning inner-child healing: identifying thoughts, feelings, and needs

Stage Three: Healing Homo-Emotional/Homo-Social Wounds (Psychodynamic Therapy)

- Continuing all tasks of Stage One and Two
- Discovering the root causes of homo-emotional/social wounds
- Beginning the process of grieving, forgiving and taking responsibility
- Developing healthy, healing same-gender relationships

Stage Four: Healing Hetero-Emotional/Hetero-Social Wounds (Psychodynamic Therapy)

- Continuing all tasks of Stage One, Stage Two and Stage Three
- Discovering the root causes of hetero-emotional/social wounds
- Continuing the process of grieving, forgiving and taking responsibility
- Developing healthy, healing opposite-sex relationships and learning about the opposite sex through the perspective of one's own gender

© Richard Cohen, M.A., 2023

This is a linear and developmental model. However, it does not work as neatly and cleanly as I am about to describe. The individual in transition may move from Stage One to Stage Three, back to Stage Two, then to Stage One again. It all depends upon the growth, maturity and needs of the individual.

The benefit of having this four-stage model is that it represents a road map of recovery. If someone jumps from Stage One to Stage Three, he will eventually need to return to the previous stage and continue to work on and work through those necessary tasks. It is like taking a road trip from New York to California. Somewhere around Chicago, he remembers a very painful experience he had as a child while living in Wisconsin. So he boards a plane, flies to Wisconsin, takes care of healing that wound, and gets back on a plane, returning once again to Chicago. Then he continues on the road from Chicago to California.

You may think, if he could fly from Chicago to Wisconsin, then why can't he just fly from New York to California and do away with the road trip altogether? There are no shortcuts in life when it comes to matters of the heart. In the process of healing, he is reclaiming his lost self, those parts of his character that he has either buried or not developed. This takes time, patience and diligent effort. The price is high to get one's life back, but the rewards are priceless. Without making this journey, I would not be alive today. Those who try to fly without doing their heart-work may end up crashing in mid-flight.

As psychotherapist Jan Frank stated, *"The process of healing goes from bad, to worse and then better"* (presentation entitled *Stages of Recovery*, PFOX conference, Fairfax, VA, 1998). People come in for counseling while in crisis; they feel very bad. As they discover the source(s) of their issue(s), things often get worse as they experience more pain. Finally, things improve when healing occurs and real love is experienced.

A word of warning to therapists, counselors, coaches, ministry leaders and caregivers: If you ever find yourself working harder, or being more invested in the therapy than your client, then something is wrong. Your job is to be the pickaxe, helping the client unearth causes for present and past issues. Your client must take up the shovel and do his/her own work if he/she is to heal. Same-Sex Attraction is an indication of delayed development, being stuck in some earlier stage or stages of psychosexual, psychosocial, psychospiritual and psychological development. Therefore, much of the work will be identifying where there is developmental arrest, helping the client heal wounds, and assisting in the fulfillment of unmet love needs. For this to occur, instruction, guidance and proper re-parenting will be necessary.

Those working with the struggler need to understand: 1) the causes of same-sex attraction; 2) the four stages of recovery; and 3) the need for the fulfillment of developmental tasks in each stage. Here is where the therapeutic tools and techniques are important. It is necessary to follow the four stages in proper order to ensure that the individual does not omit developmental tasks and jeopardize his/her success. (Again, if necessary, one may need to jump from one stage to another to take care of some immediate business, e.g., deep grieving or facing a critical situation. After this is complete, one must return to the previous stage of healing.)

A Brief Summary of the Four Stages of Recovery

Stage One: The individual needs to cut ties with gay porn, stop homosexual behavior, terminate homosexual relationships and build a strong Support Network of healthy love. He/she needs to develop a sense of self-worth through experiencing a personal relationship with God/Higher Power. This is behavioral therapy, modifying unhealthy behaviors and replacing them with positive, healthy sources of love.

Stage Two: The individual needs to develop skills to create happiness in his/her present-day relationships. This is cognitive therapy, teaching communication and problem-solving skills, assertiveness training and correcting faulty thinking. Then he/she begins inner-child work, learning about feelings and needs, and fostering self-love and compassion. If an individual bypasses this stage, chances are that he/she will terminate treatment, give up and/or revert to homosexual behavior.

Stage Three: The individual needs to identify homo-emotional/homo-social wounds, heal them, and then fulfill them in healthy, nonsexual same-gender relationships. This is the psychodynamic work of recovery, exposing the wounds, grieving the pains and losses of the past, learning to forgive, and finally moving on. The result is a renewed and empowered sense of one's true gender identity.

Stage Four: The individual needs to identify hetero-emotional/hetero-social wounds, heal them, and then fulfill them in healthy opposite-sex relationships. He needs to learn about women from a male perspective, and she needs to learn about men from a female perspective.

People always ask me how long it will take to complete the four stages of healing. It all depends on the severity of the wounds and the amount of time and energy the individual is willing to invest in his healing. One-and-a-half to three years is the average time of treatment. Our job as therapists is to equip our clients with the proper tools and skills to take care of themselves throughout their lives.

Please read Chapters Four and Six in *Being Gay* for a much more detailed explanation of the Four Stages of Healing.

The Initial Session

When someone comes for help and shares about the nature of his situation and current conflicts, the first thing I ask is, "What are your goals for our work together?" Quite often, many who seek counseling are not clear about their goals. However, they must address and answer this question. It makes them think about what they want and need, and it gives the client and the helper a clear direction for their work.

When we decide to work together, I begin by taking a thorough history. Generally, this takes from two to three hours, sometimes more. During this time, the client has an opportunity to share much about his/her life, many things that he/she has never shared with anyone before. It gives the therapist/coach a bird's-eye view of the multi-generational family system and many other contributing factors that the client will need to address along the road of recovery.

Instead of going over the history in two or three sessions, the therapist may email the client the Family History Questionnaire. Ask him/her to respond to each question succinctly, with a maximum of 8 pages. Additionally, I ask him/her to draw a genogram of three generations (examples of genograms are readily available online). I show the client an example of a genogram: beginning with paternal and maternal grandparents, the client's parents, siblings, and the families of the client and siblings (if they exist). It is very interesting to see how much the individual does or does not know about his/her parents and grandparents. This in itself may be very revealing about family relationships, or lack thereof.

PART I: BLUEPRINT FOR HEALING

Family History Questionnaire

Section One:

1. Name your father's parents (your paternal grandfather and grandmother) and name your father's siblings in birth order from oldest to youngest, including your father. Include the year that each person was born (grandparents and siblings). Identify who is/was married to whom, and who might have passed away. Also include if there were any miscarriages, stillbirths, abortions, or if a child died.
2. Name your mother's parents (your maternal grandfather and grandmother) and name your mother's siblings in birth order from oldest to youngest, including your mother. Include the year that each person was born (grandparents and siblings). Identify who is/was married to whom, and who might have passed away. Also include if there were any miscarriages, stillbirths, abortions, or if a child died.
3. Names, birth years, and children that your parents had (your siblings and you). List if your siblings are married, and their spouses' name(s), and number of children.
4. Include the age, name, and gender of each of your children (if you are married). If there was a

miscarriage, stillbirth, abortion, or a child died, please include each of them as well. List their birth order, the year they were born, and if applicable, when they passed away.

Section Two:

1. Describe the relationship between your father and his father, your father and his mother, your father and his siblings (if he had any), and your father and any other significant people in his life while he was growing up. Include the names and birth order of all your father's siblings.
2. Describe the relationship between your father's parents—past to present.
3. Where did your father's family live? Where did he grow up?
4. What was their ethnic background? What was their religious background?
5. Describe the relationship between your mother and her father, your mother and her mother, your mother and her siblings, and any other significant people in her life growing up. Include the names and birth order of all your mother's siblings.
6. Describe the relationship between your mother's parents—past to present.
7. Where did your mother's family live? Where did she grow up?

8. What was their ethnic background? Religious background?
9. Be sure to describe any major issues or events on both the paternal and maternal sides of the family, such as war experiences, immigration, sexual abuse, physical abuse, emotional-mental abuse, drug/alcohol/sexual addictions, gambling addictions, eating disorders, sexual problems, major depressions, divorce, suicide, rape, murder, theft, autism, abortions, homosexuality, adoption, moving, etc.

Section Three:

1. Describe your relationship with your father—past (from your earliest memories) to the present (current-day relationship).
2. Describe your father's personality—past to present.
3. Describe your father's education, employment history, and religious history.
4. Describe your relationship with your mother—past to present.
5. Describe your mother's personality—past to present.
6. Describe your mother's education, employment history, and religious history.
7. Describe the relationship between your father and mother—past to present.

8. Describe your relationship with your siblings (if you have any)—past to present.
9. Describe your siblings' personalities.
10. Describe your relationship with any other significant people in or out of your family system (e.g., grandmother, grandfather, uncle, cousin, neighbor, stepparent).
11. What was your role in the family system (e.g., hero, pleaser, clown, rebel, substitute spouse, golden child, caretaker, loner, scapegoat, peacemaker)?
12. Describe your school history—academically and socially, past to present.
13. Describe your sexual history—from your earliest memories to the present. Include all references to sex and sexuality, in or outside of the family. When did your homosexual feelings and desires begin?
14. Describe your history of masturbation—when it began, how it progressed, and how frequently you masturbate today. Are there any special rituals you perform while masturbating? Is masturbating accompanied by fantasies and pornography? If so, please describe what images you like to view?
15. Describe your sexual fantasies—from past to present, as they may have progressed over time. What kind of person/people are you attracted to? What are his or her characteristics (physical attributes and personality traits)? What activities are performed in your fantasies and in

what environment? Do you have any particular fetishes? If so, please describe them, when they started, and how they manifest in your life today.
16. Describe your religious history—past to present.
17. Describe yourself—how you see yourself today.
18. List any other significant issues about your life or your family that were not covered in these questions, such as health issues, marriage issues, extramarital affairs, career issues, money issues, and previous treatment or therapy.
19. How do you feel about your body? Are you pleased with how you look? Has this changed over time?
20. List your current and past employment history, and your age.
21. Please list your goals for the therapy.

One thing that becomes apparent while reviewing the client's family history is the generational detachment between same-gender parents and their same-gender children, e.g., the distance between fathers and sons, and mothers and daughters. I have observed in many of my male clients' weaker paternal figures and much stronger maternal figures. This leads a male to identify more easily with the feminine, the stronger of the sexes in the family system.

While sharing about his family history, one client stated, "I wanted to be a girl because my father liked my sister more than me. He was always working and while at home he was angry. My mother was more fun, could speak her mind and was more loving."

It is important to have him/her share about his/her earliest childhood memories because it is the fertile soil that cultivates future SSA. Pay close attention to memory lapses—there is much useful information locked in the unconscious. *The conscious mind cannot hold that which was too painful to remember.* These places will be important to revisit when working through stages three and four of recovery.

When reviewing the individual's social life during school years, I most often hear "I'm different," "I don't belong," and "I don't fit in." Inquiring about sexual fantasies or fetishes is important. There is much useful information here since the homo-emotional/homo-social wounds hide beneath the fantasies/fetishes. There is generally a progression of fantasies as well. Sometimes it starts by just observing naked men or women, and then progresses to sexual activity. This will be unique to each individual, depending upon the specific needs and intensity of detachment from self and others.

Some feel attracted to older men, displaying a need to be taken care of or fathered. Some adolescents and adult males feel attracted to peers, seeking in other men what they feel lacking within themselves. Most men feel drawn to muscular, strong and confident men—all the qualities they wish to possess. Some want to feel dominated, held, cared for or mentored by the men they admire. Others have an attraction to younger boys or teens. This may represent several things: 1) unresolved trauma at that particular age; 2) unmet needs in that stage of development; and/or 3) a connection to some form of abuse at that age (oftentimes a repressed or suppressed memory of sexual abuse).

It is important to realize that sexual fantasies are a mask for unmet homo-emotional/homo-social love needs or fear of intimacy with someone of the opposite sex. I have also found that these fantasies may hide repressed anger toward one or both parents, anger that the child felt unable to express and is now being manifest as sexual desires. Still others, disconnected from their own sense of gender identity, want to watch heterosexual men having sexual relations with women. In this way, they find their lost identities in the men they wish to be. There are many variations of sexual fantasies. It is important to find out as much detail as possible in order to understand the deeper meanings behind their SSA.

It is important to see what part religion has played in the client's life and what role it now plays. Many experienced judgement and/or persecution within their particular faith. I have heard horror stories of how they sought help from their clergy and were then asked to leave the congregation. Others feared to reveal their struggle because of the strong judgmental attitudes of those in their faith. In other cases, if they have strongly detached from their parents, then they may easily detach from their parents' religious beliefs. **Oppositional behavior is an integral part of SSA.** One young client shared with me, "I consciously chose to be different from my father. If he liked country music, I chose rock. If he liked white, I chose black. This was my way of telling him that I didn't like him at all."

After reading the client's responses, I write an evaluation or content analysis, offering my observations and hypotheses why I believe he/she experiences SSA, based on the ten potential causes. When I present this evaluation/content analysis to the clients, I invite them to first listen. If I have made a mistake or misperceived something, I ask him/her to correct me. This is generally a positive and deeply moving experience for the client. Finally, someone truly understands him/her from the inside out. There are often many tears during this session. "No one has ever understood me so deeply before."

After completing the evaluation, I also give him/her a personalized treatment plan based on the four stages of healing (see an example of a treatment plan in our *Clinician's Handbook: Assisting Our LGBTQ+ Loved Ones*). Then we begin therapy. If a client is in extreme pain at the initial session or sessions, please give him/her time to express his/her feelings and thoughts before doing a thorough history. This may be the first time for him/her to have found a safe space to let go and release his/her pain and frustration. The therapist, counselor or coach must create a sacred setting that is confidential, safe and nonjudgmental.

PART I: BLUEPRINT FOR HEALING

Four Stages of Resolving Unwanted Same-Sex Attraction

Stage One: Transition / Behavioral Therapy

- Cutting off from sexual activity: playgrounds, playmates, playthings
- Developing a Support Network
- Building self-worth and experiencing value in relationship with God/Higher Power

SUPPORT NETWORK

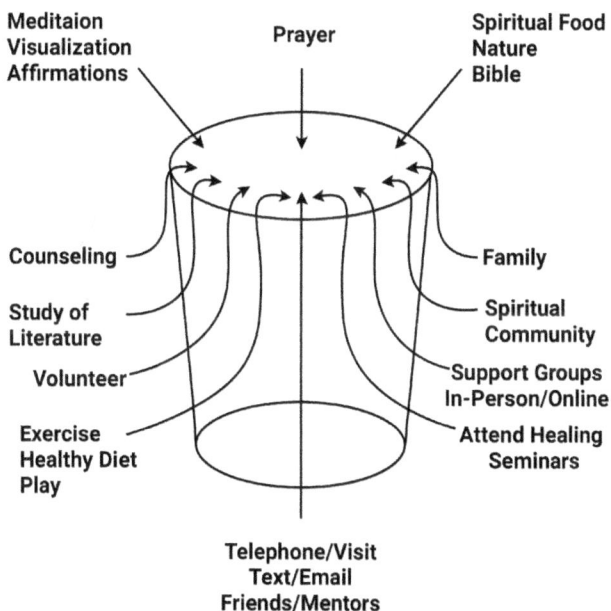

Richard Cohen, M.A. © 2023

In Stage One, the individual seeks help to resolve his/her unwanted SSA. Perhaps the client tried to suppress his/her homosexual feelings unsuccessfully. Perhaps he/she married, hoping his/her SSA would disappear, but alas it has not. Perhaps after trying to find Mr. Right or Ms. Right, he or she feels empty and alone. Perhaps he/she is young and confused about his/her gender identity or sexual orientation. Perhaps SSA is in conflict with their spiritual beliefs. The success of therapy is predicated upon a heartfelt motivation for change. It does not matter if the individual is thirteen or seventy, change *is* possible at any age.

The first task in Stage One is to cut off from playgrounds, playmates and playthings: places where they met other gay-active persons, people with whom they engaged in homosexual behavior, and porn/other erotic homosexual materials. Of course, this won't happen overnight, it will take time. In some cases, struggles with compulsive behaviors may persist even as a client completes other tasks and progresses into subsequent stages. Encourage your client to be patient with himself or herself. It takes time to build a healthy internal ego-structure and an external support system.

Therefore, the second task in Stage One is to develop a substantial Support Network. The central organizing factor(s) in the life of anyone who experiences SSA may be homosexual relationships, sexual fantasies, compulsive masturbation, porn and/or hangouts (gay bars, baths, parks, etc.). It is insufficient to simply tell someone to cut off from these relationships and behaviors. It is essential to realize that these playgrounds, playmates and playthings represent unhealthy attempts to fulfill legitimate needs for love. Only healthy, healing, nonsexual relationships will serve him or her in restoring their broken heart.

A Support Network must be developed to provide a nurturing environment for your client to heal, grow and mature. Healthy nonsexual relationships with those of the same gender, and healthy behaviors will now replace sexual activities and/or fantasies. The Support Network represents his/her new family of choice. It may consist of, but not be limited to, his relationship with God, prayer, family, friends, spouse (if he/she is married), spiritual community, support groups, mentors and friends, online and/or in-person support groups, exercise, healthy diet, sports, games, therapeutic massage, study of healing literature, counseling and volunteer work.

Developing such a comprehensive network of support will take time and effort. Your client may seek the assistance of family, friends, a spiritual director, online groups, and a therapist in this process. Unless such a Support Network is created, they will not be able to move on to the other stages of healing. If they attempt to continue their healing work without doing this critical task, all other efforts are most likely to fail, as they will have no one to support them when they begin the process of grief.

What occurred in hurtful relationships must be healed in healthy relationships.

"As we have seen, central to the repairing of homosexuality is the establishment of nonsexual intimate relationships with men. Same-sex friendships have shown themselves to be therapeutic in the lives of men who, without psychotherapy, discovered their own ways of dealing with homosexuality" Joseph Nicolosi Sr., *Reparative Therapy of Male Homosexuality: A New Clinical Approach* (Northvale, NJ: Jason Aronson, Inc., 1991, Liberal Mind Publishers, updated edition, 2020), 194.

The third task of Stage One is to build a sense of self-worth and experience a loving relationship with God/Higher Power. This is not a religious exercise. It is prescribed for the client to develop a deeply personal connection to a loving Creator. He/she needs to internalize the truth that he/she is profoundly loved and accepted, SSA and all.

I have my clients write a list of affirmations, things they wish their parents, siblings and peers would have said and done with them while growing up. Once the lists are reviewed by the therapist, the client finds mentors/ friends to make a recording of the affirmations. I suggest that she or he listens to these affirmations daily for a minimum of six months. This will have dramatic and positive results. Read more details about affirmations on pages 176-180 in *Being Gay: Nature, Nurture or Both*? "Filling our minds with positive images of wellbeing, can produce an epigenetic environment that reinforces the healing process," Dawson Church, *The Genie in Your Genes: Epigenetic Medicine and the New Biology of Intention*, (Santa Rosa, CA: Elite Books, 2007), 69.

Alex was the youngest of four children. His older brother was Jason, and his older sisters were Becky and Sarah, respectively. He lived in Ohio where his father worked for a large corporation and his mother was a housewife. Alex never got along well with his dad. His father was prone to outbursts of anger, especially when he drank, which increased as Alex got older. His mother would lament about her disappointments with her husband while holding Alex in her arms. A hypersensitive child by nature, Alex experienced her pain and suffering as though it were his own. More and more, Alex aligned himself with his mother and grew to hate his neglectful and abusive father.

Jason was the athlete of the family. He was a natural at baseball, basketball and football. Alex felt that he could never measure up to Jason's athletic prowess. As his mom's favorite, he was more inclined to the arts and reading. He would watch as Jason and his friends played sports, wishing that he, too, was just one of the guys. Alex played with his sisters and felt more comfortable in their world. When his dad saw him playing games with his sisters, he called him a "faggot" and "sissy." "You're going to grow up to be one of the girls," his dad would comment. He never spent any quality time with his son. When at home, his dad hid behind the newspaper or watched TV. Often, he would not come home until late. He was out drinking with his buddies.

Alex began to experience SSA in the last few years of elementary school. He always envied the boys who were more athletic and competent. He longed to be just like them. (Dr. Nicolosi, Sr. would characterize this as the "kitchen window boy.") During puberty, those feelings became eroticized as he imagined having sexual relations with the classmates he admired. He dared not share those thoughts and feelings with his family. His dad already considered him a sissy, and his brother would frequently beat him up. Jason and his dad had an antagonistic relationship. They related through arguments and fistfights. Alex wanted no part of that, so he remained an outsider, alone in his fantasies about men.

A neighbor introduced Alex to masturbation, and eventually they became frequent sex partners. Alex felt ashamed of these activities. He and his family attended church weekly. He knew that homosexual behavior was wrong (according to his spiritual beliefs), but his feelings were so strong. The guilt

PART I: BLUEPRINT FOR HEALING

was tremendous, but his need for male intimacy was greater. The relationship with the neighbor continued throughout middle school until he moved away. Then Alex found male pornography and began to masturbate several times a day.

Alex had sex with several other classmates while in high school. They were all short-term relationships, as Alex continued to battle these desires. In college, he began to have anonymous sex with men in parks, bathrooms and bathhouses. He was an honors student majoring in business and eventually law. Alex had a very sharp mind and was admired by most of his classmates, but no one knew that Alex led a double life. By day, he was the clever, brilliant student. By night, he was a sex addict, seeking yet another man to fill his empty soul and relieve his loneliness and pain.

When I began to counsel Alex, he was in his late twenties and a very successful lawyer making an excellent salary. But Alex was miserable. His colleagues admired his brilliant mind, his way with words, and his successful trial skills. But Alex hated himself. He longed to be one of the guys. He felt like he was on the outside looking in. He felt ashamed of his addictions to anonymous sex, male pornography and compulsive masturbation. He wanted out, but he did not know how to change.

At first, I had Alex fill out the family history questionnaire. After reviewing his history, I presented him with an evaluation and treatment plan. We then began our therapeutic relationship. I had Alex read several books about the etiology of same-sex attraction. Gradually, he began to understand where these desires originated. He understood that he had emotionally detached from his father and had an unhealthy attachment with his mother. Being more sensitive, he feared his father and the strength that he represented. Rather than standing up to his dad, he ran for safety into the arms of his mother and sisters. He came to see that his sexual exploits were a mask for the unobtained love and affection from his father and his inability to communicate his needs in a positive and assertive manner.

Alex was hungry to learn and grow. The next task was to help him build a strong Support Network in order to replace the sexual addictions with healthy, healing relationships. He was fearful about sharing his struggle with others. He had managed to isolate this part of his life since he began experiencing SSA. I gently encouraged him to join a support group of other men in the process of transitioning. He resisted until I told him that in order for me to help him, I needed him to join such a group. Finally, he agreed to attend a meeting. There, to his great surprise, he met other men just like himself who had suffered their entire lives with similar feelings and experiences. He was so relieved and so grateful to learn that he was not alone. He met others who understood him.

Alex began an exercise program. He joined a gym and worked out with men who were secure in their sexuality. As Alex had always been on the sidelines watching his brother and other boys, it was scary for him to participate in group sports. He sought a mentor to teach him basic athletic skills: throwing the ball, hitting the ball, catching the ball, and shooting hoops. Over a period of time, he began to experience his own strength and power. (A word of caution: I encourage those coming out of homosexuality to find *family-oriented* health clubs and exercise with OSA friends.)

He also made his own affirmation MP3 to reinforce his sense of self-worth. I had him write a list of affirmations, things that he wished his dad and others had said to him while growing up. Alex had a mentor and several friends make the recording. It was just about five minutes in length with soothing music in the background. Some of the affirmations were: "Alex, I love you for who you are." "You are my precious son." "You are enough." "You are talented, gifted and strong." "I believe in you." "We want you to hang out with us." By using these affirmations on a daily basis, Alex began to believe in his value and self-worth as a beloved son of God.

He began to redefine himself. No longer was he a homosexual man, but a precious son of God. Gradually, Alex began to understand that he did not have to earn love and acceptance through appearance or outward success. He was simply loved for who he was. This was a revelation for Alex. This internal transformation, combined with new social skills, his support group, and weekly counseling, gave him the strength to stop acting out sexually. Occasionally, he would have a sexual experience, but they were decreasing each week.

Stage Two: Grounding / Cognitive Therapy

- Continuing with the Support Network
- Continuing to build self-worth and experience value in relationship with God
- Building skills: assertiveness training, communication skills, and problem-solving techniques
- Beginning inner-child healing: identifying thoughts, feelings and needs

The first and second tasks of Stage Two are for the clients to continue building and participating in their Support Network, use their affirmations daily, and experience being loved as a precious son or daughter of God, SSA and all. One does not need to resolve his or her SSA in order to be loved by God.

The third task of Stage Two is to equip the client with communication skills for both sharing and listening (see the *Clinician's Handbook: Assisting Our LGBTQ+ Loved Ones*). This helps them become more assertive, honest and real in personal and professional relationships. We begin to apply Cognitive Behavioral skills as written about in David Burns's *Ten Days to Self-Esteem* (New York: William Morrow and Company, 1999), or *Mind Over Mood: Change How You Feel by Changing the Way You Think*, Dennis Greenberger and Christine A. Padesky (New York: Gullford Press, 2015). I have them do one chapter every two weeks; additionally, they will practice doing 3-4 Daily Mood Logs weekly. Through applying these simple and effective techniques on a daily basis, they will slay cognitive distortions and incorporate more loving, truthful messages into their mind and heart. Once again, the field of Neuroplasticity demonstrates that the more we practice positive affirmations and loving thoughts about ourselves and others, our neural pathways will change for good!

For over fifteen years I led a support group for those who experienced unwanted SSA. One of the many mantras that I taught my clients was this: *Life is not a popularity contest, it's a come-as-you-are party!* In other words, be who you are—some will like you, others will not. Many who experience unwanted SSA are the pleasers, always amending their personalities for the approval of others. I taught them that this codependent behavior compromises who they genuinely are, as a powerful man or woman.

The fourth task of Stage Two is beginning the work of inner child healing. The term "inner child" is synonymous with the unconscious. I have the client do all the exercises in *Recovery of Your Inner Child*, Lucia

Capacchione (New York: Touchstone Publisher/Simon & Schuster, 1999). I ask them to do one chapter every two weeks (using a sketch pad, colored pencils and crayons). Now they uncover the wounded child within, and become a more loving, protective and nurturing parent to their own soul. Additionally, I have them listen to inner child meditations that I created (https://www.pathinfo.org/digital-downloads). There are many other wonderful inner child meditations available online.

> Alex attended his support group weekly. It gave him a sense of stability and camaraderie that he needed as he continued his healing journey. Alex always told me that a life-changing concept for him was that homosexuality was not the problem but a *symptom* of unresolved issues. He stated that this concept freed him to take the focus off of his sexuality and to deal with the underlying causes of his same-sex attraction. We continued to meet weekly for therapy. I had him begin using Dr. David Burns's book, *Ten Days to Self-Esteem*. Reluctantly, he began doing the assignments. Like many others that I have counseled, Alex did not like this workbook. "It reminds me of all the homework assignments I had to do for school." I told him, "I understand your resistance, and it is fine to dislike it. Just do it anyway." And he did.
>
> By practicing Burns's methods, Alex learned to identify his negative self-talk and cognitive distortions

that led him into a vicious cycle of depression and sexual addiction. By doing the Daily Mood Logs and other activities suggested by Burns, he gained a greater sense of how his thoughts led to negative feelings. Then, instead of getting upset with himself and others, he took the time to reflect on his negative thinking and transform those thoughts into positive energy. This was yet another way in which he gained greater self-awareness and power over the addictive cycle. Dr. Douglas Weiss describes the addictive cycle by the following six stages: 1) Pain agents—emotional discomfort, unresolved conflict, stress, or a need to connect, 2) Disassociation, 3) The altered state, 4) Pursuing behavior, 5) Behavior, and 6) Guilt and shame.

Alex continued to meditate either daily or several times per week, using the inner child and healing meditations that I created. He continued listening to his Affirmations every morning and evening, sometimes while driving to and from work.

By participating in sports and exercise, Alex was strengthening his masculinity as well. After working with his sports mentor for months, he finally built up the courage to begin playing basketball with some other men. It was very frightening for him at first. He used the cognitive techniques, slaying negative self-talk with positive and rational responses. It was difficult for him to do this. He used creative visualization, imagining that he was a competent, accomplished basketball player already. He practiced visualizing this several times throughout the day. He decided upon a new goal each time he played basketball. One time his goal was to just have fun, no matter how he played. Another time his goal was to focus on skill building—dribbling and passing the ball. Another time his goal was to be as assertive as possible. He also asked a friend to practice with him. Through his continued efforts, his game gradually improved and he learned to have fun.

After completing Burns's cognitive therapy, he began inner-child healing. Alex did the assignments in Dr. Lucia Capacchione's book, *Recovery of Your Inner Child*. As a lawyer, he found this approach ridiculous and stupid. "What does drawing pictures with my opposite hand have to do with resolving my SSA? This seems absurd!" Again, I told Alex, "It's fine to dislike it. Just do it." And so he did. At first, the inner-child drawing and dialogue exercises were very difficult for him. It was slow going. Getting in touch with the inner voice was a painstaking process for Alex. For so many years, he had buried that hurt little boy beneath all the good grades, smiles, pleasantries, and sexual activity. But through his consistent and concerted efforts, eventually the child within (his unconscious) began to speak.

Alex was shocked at what began to emerge—a very angry and raging little boy. He was not nice.

He was not sweet. He was hurt, and he wanted to be heard. And so, Alex completed many drawings and allowed the little boy within to voice his feelings. During several sessions, I created exercises for that particular inner child. He did some Bioenergetic work, pounding on pillows with a tennis racquet. Learn about this therapeutic modality in *Bioenergetics* by Alexander Lowen (https://www.lowenfoundation.org/what-is-bioenergetics). No longer was Alex the sweet, submissive child, but a strong and powerful, masculine force.

He also tapped into other parts of his inner family—the protective parent, the frightened little boy, the critical parent, the playful child. Alex was awakening parts of himself that had been dormant for years. He was learning to access feelings, thoughts and needs he never knew he had. Alex used the meditation MP3, *Healing Your Inner Child*, several times a week. Through these inner-child healing activities, he began to find his emotional center and become more powerfully aware of who he was rather than seeking to define himself in response to how others thought and felt about him.

Stage Three: Healing Homo-Emotional and Homo-Social Wounds / Psychodynamic Therapy

- Continuing all tasks of Stage One and Stage Two
- Discovering, working through the root causes of homo-emotional and/or homo-social wounds
- Beginning/continuing the process of grieving, forgiving and taking responsibility
- Developing/continuing healthy, healing nonsexual same-gender relationships

The first task in Stage Three is to continue with one's Support Network, affirmations, communication skills, cognitive-behavior tools/techniques, and inner child healing exercises and meditations.

The second task of Stage Three is a growing awareness of the same-gender parent wounds (father-son or mother-daughter) and wounding with any other same gender persons during childhood and adolescence. I have the client write a list of his or her homo-emotional and homo-social wounds that need to be reconciled and resolved. *Feelings buried alive never die.* We are condemned to repeat the past until we face, trace, erase and resolve each issue.

The third task of Stage Three is the process of grieving, forgiving and assuming responsibility. As a psychotherapist, I use a variety of therapeutic techniques and modalities, e.g., Family Systems Therapy, Bibliotherapy,

Psycho-education, Somatic therapeutic techniques (Bio-energetics, EMDR, EFT), Role Play (Gestalt Therapy), NLP (Neuro-Linguistic Programing), Focusing, Voice Dialogue, Transactional Analysis, Journaling. Please read pages 160–165 in Chapter Six of *Being Gay*. There are many other therapeutic protocols listed in our *Clinician's Handbook: Assisting Our LGBTQ+ Loved Ones* that are useful for individual, couples and group therapy.

The above-mentioned modalities are not an exhaustive list of techniques that you may use, they are merely some of the methods that I have found efficacious. As the field of psychology is ever changing, you may learn about and practice newer techniques. My main point for therapists is this: An individual must pass through the four stages of healing in order to reconcile and resolve his or her unwanted SSA. Therapeutic techniques are always changing and improving, however the path of recovery remains the same as this is a developmental condition.

This next section is written by a brilliant psychiatrist and psychotherapist living and practicing in the Middle East. I mentored him for many years. He has helped numerous clients resolve their unwanted SSA. He is now training and teaching other therapists how to do this work.

Trauma Focused Perspective

ShehabEldeen K.A., M.D.

First of all, it is worth stating that this is not a change-oriented but a healing-oriented approach to therapy. Change is a personal decision. The role of the therapist is to empower the client in fulfilling his/her stated goals of treatment. Trauma Focused Therapy, with its understanding that past disturbances sculpt the very nature of who we are in the present, uses a very delicate approach. It is not uncovering the wounds of the past, as it may destabilize the present moment, but attaining so carefully the living legacy of trauma buried in the body and soul. Trauma research reveals that much of what is thought to be "normal" is in fact a trauma reaction, and that one does not have to live with it. Old coping mechanisms may be resolved and new cognitive and behavioral patterns attained.

What is trauma and why is it crucial to understand how it is affecting one's life? Trauma as a broad term includes any adverse life experience that was too distressing for one's brain to process as a memory, especially the developing brain of a child. It could have been as simple as a prolonged incubation period after birth, being raised by a depressed mother or a rageaholic father, a teasing sibling, or other factually traumatizing events such as sexual abuse. The traumatic event is still very alive in the here and now either by itself (e.g., flash backs) or through its effects (e.g., dissociation, coping strategies). Hence, we talk about developmental trauma, attachment trauma, psycho-cultural trauma, sexual trauma, and so on.

What makes an event a traumatic one? I distinguish three main contributing factors in this context:

1) *The threshold of the event itself*: war, rape, and physical abuse are traumatic by themselves, and they are called big Ts in the field of trauma.
2) *The complexity of the response needed*: when the event puts a burden on the experiencing subject to take two-or-more moves in different directions; fight and flight at the same time, and/or flee, and take care of someone else at the same time, or when the event charges the subject with two opposing, complex emotions such as love/hate as in incest or seduction.
3) **When the brain itself is not able to process the event**: as in the child's developing brain, and when the experiencing subject is already distressed or escalated by other distressing factors.

We take into consideration that trauma controls one's life through many things; the most important of them are dissociative experiences and adaptive strategies—that can be a whole lifestyle—and both were essential to survive the past and keep one captive in the present. In Trauma Focused Therapy, we do not dig into the client's history to uncover his/her trauma; on the contrary, we use a very delicate and cautious manner to deal with the legacy that left behind what happened in his/her body, psyche, and spirit.

Trauma focused therapy is divided into three core stages:

1) **Stabilization**: The therapy aims at increasing the client's distress tolerance, "widening his *window of tolerance*," decreasing the automatic dissociative tendencies, bringing the adaptive strategies into awareness, increasing confidence and empowerment, being mindful of the here and now, and ceasing of life threatening and quality of life degrading behaviors.

2) **Processing**: This can be metaphorically described as digesting the adverse event, and being aware that trauma isn't defined by what happened, but how our brains handled that event. After this stage, adverse experiences will still be perceived as adverse experiences but will not be traumatizing any longer. The client will be set free from past coping strategies. Here we do not treat the event per se, but how the client experienced it, and how it affected his/her life physically, mentally, emotionally and/or spiritually.

3) **Integration**: Here therapy aims at post-traumatic growth, and at making use of the trauma legacy

in his/her mental, psychological, and spiritual growth.

Many different modalities are built around the same principles; hence they are called Trauma Focused Therapies. Modalities that target traumatic experiences can be divided into two categories:

- **Trauma focused (tf) conventional therapies**, i.e., trauma focused Cognitive Behavioral Therapy (tfCBT), Dialectical Behavioral Therapy (DBT), Emotionally Focused Therapy (EFT), and trauma focused Acceptance and Commitment Therapy (tfACT).
- **Non-conventional trauma focused therapies**, i.e., Psychodrama, Internal Family Systems, and Somatic experiencing therapy.

Once again, the above section was authored by a brilliant psychiatrist/psychotherapist living and practicing in the Middle East.

The fourth task of Stage Three is continuing with his/her Support Network, especially with healthy same-gender friends and mentors. They will prove to be essential in this stage of recovery as he/she will need their profound presence as they grieve the many wounds of their past. In this process, the hurts will be replaced by healthy love and healthy touch. More about the indelible need for healthy touch in a moment.

A THERAPIST'S GUIDE

LAYERS OF OUR PERSONALITY

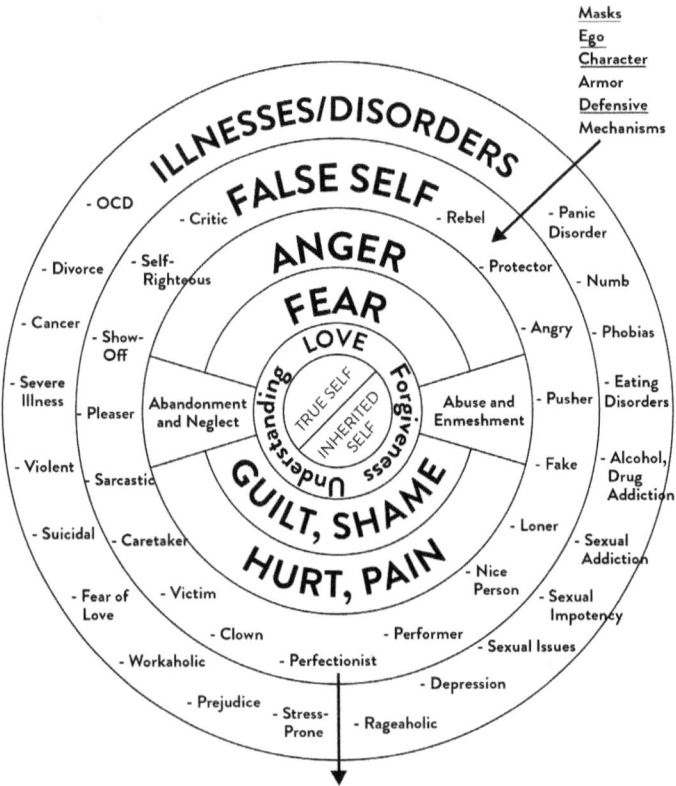

Affection, Affirmation, Acceptance

Richard Cohen, M.A. © 2023

PART I: BLUEPRINT FOR HEALING

A detailed explanation about the Layers of Our Personality is on pages 121–125 in *Being Gay*. This chart helps to explain how healing occurs in the heart, mind and body of the individual.

> Alex understood the root causes of his SSA and was ready to face the past, heal the wounds, and fulfill unmet love needs. His sexual addictions to anonymous sex, male pornography, and compulsive masturbation were no longer a part of his daily life. He had friends, played sports, used his affirmation MP3, prayed and meditated, and had developed a strong sense of his inherent value as a beloved son of God. He practiced good communication skills in his personal and professional life. Whenever someone spoke hurtful words, he would either take care of himself or he would share honestly with the other person. *Healing is about being straightforward with self and others.*
>
> Now it was time to delve into the past. Through Voice Dialogue, Focusing, EFT, Bioenergetics, Role Play and Inner Child work, we began to explore the pain Alex experienced in relationship to his father and brother. *Restoration works in reverse to the way in which the original wounding occurred.* First, one must deal with the lesser wound before facing the more profound wound. Alex sensed that, first, he needed to heal with Jason. Through Role Play and

Voice Dialogue, he allowed his wounded inner child to come forth and share with Jason how he felt when attacked and beaten. Frozen tears and primal emotions were released as Alex's inner child spoke about his pain. "Why did you hit me? Why did you beat me? I needed your love so much, but all I felt was your anger."

We also used Bioenergetic exercises to allow his inner child to express his anger and pain. I had him imagine Jason standing on the other side of the pillows as he screamed, pounded, and eventually took back his power. Alex had, in a most unhealthy manner, submitted to Jason and his dad. He abdicated responsibility by shutting down emotionally, thus becoming a "victim." During several sessions, while utilizing memory healing, Alex was able to grieve the loss of a close relationship with his brother, experience relief, and ultimately forgive Jason. Through healing his own wounds, he was able to see the common wounding in Jason, who was equally deficient in experiencing healthy father's love. Through Role Play, Voice Dialogue, Focusing, Bioenergetics, Memory Healing, EFT and Inner Child exercises, Alex was able to reclaim a part of his masculinity.

Next, it was time to investigate his relationship with his father. Alex allowed his inner child to share with his dad how he felt when he was verbally, emotionally, and mentally abused. Again, through Role

PART I: BLUEPRINT FOR HEALING

Play, Voice Dialogue, Bioenergetics and Memory Healing, Alex grieved about the pain and loss of his father's love. "Why weren't you there for me? Where were you? I needed you. I'm not a sissy. I'm a boy, and I am deserving of your love." Alex pounded so hard, screaming, shouting, reclaiming his power, and taking back the male energy he abandoned so many years ago. "I am a boy. I am a man. I am deserving of love. I won't take your verbal abuse anymore. I give you back all your shame, all your name-calling, all your fears and guilt."

Alex learned to stand in his power, *transitioning from a victim to a victor of love.* As he let go of his anger, frustration and pain, he began to experience more power within himself. Through memory healing, he was able to forgive his father and see the wounded child within his dad. Realizing that his father did not experience the warmth and encouragement of his own father, Alex was able to feel more compassionate and forgiving toward him.

Simultaneous with this process of inner healing, Alex was being mentored by an elder in his church. He met weekly with his mentor, Rich. They spent time together sharing. Rich was a good listener and a strong role model of masculinity. When Alex was grieving, Rich would hold him in his arms, allowing him to feel loved as he detoxed from years of repressed anger and pain. Rich was very patient and loving toward Alex. In this way, Alex's neurology was being reprogrammed. The pain was being weeded out of his system and love was being poured in—pulling weeds and planting seeds. Alex and Rich also went to games together, played ball and took walks. Alex was making up for all the times he had missed with his dad.

Alex also maintained close friendships with several guys from the gym, his support group, and his church. He was able to freely share with them what he was experiencing in his emotional and mental reprocessing work. His Support Network surrounded him as he released past pains, and reclaimed his masculinity. More and more, he felt grounded in his power. His same-sex attractions waned now that he experienced his own sense of gender identity.

Stage Four: Healing Hetero-Emotional and Hetero-Social Wounds / Psychodynamic Therapy

- Continuing all tasks of Stages One, Stage Two and Stage Three
- Discovering, working through the root causes of hetero-emotional and/or hetero-social wounds
- Continuing the process of grieving, forgiving and taking responsibility
- Developing healthy, healing opposite-sex relationships and learning to understand and appreciate

the opposite-sex through the perspective of one's own gender

The first task in Stage Four is to continue with the Support Network, affirmations, Daily Mood Logs, inner child healing activities and meditations, resolution of wounding with same-gender parents, peers and others of the same gender.

The second and third task in Stage Four is working through the root causes of wounding between mothers and sons, fathers and daughters, and any other hurts incurred by those of the opposite sex. You may utilize the same therapeutic modalities as in Stage Three.

The fourth task in Stage Four is developing healthy, healing relationships with opposite-sex mentors and friends. If the man in recovery was close to his mother, and more in touch with his feminine side, he knew women from a female perspective. The same holds true for a woman who experiences SSA. She may have known men from a more masculine point of view, not from a woman's perspective. Therefore, it is important to learn about the opposite sex in a healthy way, from the perspective of one's own gender. This is a radical shift in outlook for the person in recovery.

> "Jung said something disturbing about this complication. He said that when the son is introduced primarily by the mother to feelings, he will

learn the female attitude toward masculinity and takes a female view of his own father and of his own masculinity. He will see his father through his mother's eyes" Robert Bly, *Iron John: A Book About Men* (New York: Vintage Books, 1990), 24.

Now, the men must learn to see women from a masculine perspective, and women learn to see men from a feminine perspective. Having opposite-sex mentors and friends will be critical to helping him or her heal while grieving the painful memories and experiences that he or she had during the critical early stages of development, e.g., mother wounds for him, father wounds for her, and/or any other significant wounding experienced with/from members of the opposite sex.

Natural desires for opposite-sex relationships often emerge as he/she experiences his/her gender identity, heals hetero-emotional/hetero-social wounds, and establishes healthy relationships with members of the opposite sex. A married man will experience greater intimacy with his wife once he has healed the opposite-sex wounds of his past. A married woman will now experience greater intimacy with her husband.

The individual's true gender identity will emerge after dismantling the defensive detachments between men and men, men and women, women and women, and women and men, bonding with both the same and opposite genders. Natural attractions and feelings for the opposite sex arise out of this process of healing. There is no magic except for the profound relationships of love that arise during this process of transformation and the freedom experienced by lifting the veils of detachment.

Alex needed to work on the relationship with his mother. He had been enmeshed with her since he could remember. (*Enmeshed* describes an unhealthy attachment in an intimate relationship, whereby the proper boundaries between mother and son were violated.) He was her precious little boy, sweetheart, and substitute spouse. He carried the scars of this unhealthy attachment through his adolescence and adult life. He feared intimacy with women, afraid he would be consumed by their demands. It was time to face the mother of his past that lived deep within his soul. We used Role Play, Psychodrama, Inner Child Healing, Voice Dialogue, Bioenergetics, EFT, Memory Healing, and Family Therapy. In sessions, Alex debriefed how he felt when his mother would share her burdens with him. Through Role Play and Bioenergetics, he expressed much sadness, anger, and pain. In our support group, he created a Psychodrama, having different people play the roles of his mother, father, brother, sisters, and himself. This was a very powerful method for him to recall the family system and see what part he played in the drama and how each family member might have felt.

Alex began a mentoring relationship with Elizabeth, Rich's wife. In this way, he began to know women from another perspective. Elizabeth was neither clinging nor demanding. She simply embraced him physically and emotionally, allowing him to be a part of her and her husband's world. This was a great healing for Alex. He had never experienced what it felt like to be close to a woman in a nonthreatening way. His inner child was both scared and excited to know a woman without fear of being consumed by her needs. Elizabeth was a very refreshing influence in Alex's new life.

We arranged for Alex's parents and siblings to attend a Family Healing Session that lasted two days (I learned this therapeutic modality from Dr. Martha Welch of Columbia University; you may learn more about this protocol from our *Family Healing Session* film series and manual: https://www.pathinfo.org/fhs-film-series-manual). My wife assisted me, as she often did with Family Healing Sessions. In this way, both men and women feel represented and safer. First, Alex's parents held hands and looked into each other's eyes. I had them express how they thought and felt about one another, the good points as well as the bad points. In the beginning, they were quite superficial, playing the sweet and loving couple. Then, Jason, Alex and their sisters ganged up on each side of them and began sharing, "Stop acting so sweet. We know that each one of you is so hurt by the other. Let it out and stop making us feel like we have to take care of you!" This was a wake-up call for Alex's mom and dad. While holding her husband, his mother began to express years of pain and disappointment. She cried and screamed how lonely she was while he was out drinking. She told him how hurt she was that he had neglected and abused the children. She mourned in his arms while all the children were crying.

Next, it was Dad's turn. Still an alcoholic, he was unable to access his deeper feelings. For so many years, he had repressed his wounded self. He recalled to his wife and children how his own father had beaten him senseless, day after day, year after year, and never gave him one word of encouragement. He told them that he knew he had failed them, but at least he didn't hurt them as badly as his father had hurt him. They were all silent and shocked, as he had never shared about his family of origin before. They could see that he had masked his own pain through alcohol and overworking.

We then had Mom and Dad hold the children—first was Jason, then Becky and Sarah. Finally, it was Alex's turn. First, Alex was held by his mother. He screamed and cried, telling her how disgusted he was when she would share her misery with him. "I felt like your husband, not your son. Why did you share that crap with me? I didn't want to know your pain; I just needed your love. I never felt safe with you, only burdened and pained." He continued, "Mom, I am now establishing a new relationship with you. I need clear boundaries. I do not want to hear about your pain, your problems and your issues. I am your son, not your friend. Please get a life. Find others your own age who can help you. That's not my role. I'm your son. I need you to care for *me*." Alex felt relieved after sharing these thoughts, feelings and needs with his mom.

Alex's mom was deeply saddened by his sharing. She had no idea that he felt so hurt and betrayed. She thought she had done the best for him and the other children. She cried and apologized for any hurt she had caused her son. She told him that she loved him and that she would try not to share her burdens with him. She then went into a "poor me" mode, saying that no one is there for her. All the kids held her and shouted, "Mom, get a life. Find friends that can help and love you. Stop leaning on us!" This was very hard for her to hear.

At last, it was time for Alex to be held by his dad. Alex screamed and cried, as this was the first time for him to touch and be touched by his father. He cried out, like a child, "Dad, I missed you my whole life. Do you think I wanted to have sex with other men? I was always searching for you in their arms. I need you, Dad, I need you. Where were you? Why did you always criticize me and call me names? Please hold me and tell me that you love me." On and on he went, letting his dad know how much he was hurt by his actions and words. Alex did not want to let go of his dad since this was their first bonding experience. His father apologized for his critical nature and verbal abuse. He told Alex he was sorry that he had not been a better dad. Finally, he told his son, "I love you, Alex."

Finally, we had the kids hold hands and debrief about unresolved issues they had with one another. Jason and the girls held one another and cried as they recalled many episodes. Finally, Alex and Jason held each other. Alex told Jason how hurt and offended he was by the verbal and physical abuse. Jason apologized, knowing that he had passed on to Alex what he felt about his dad. They held each other, cried and forgave one other.

I would like to say that they all lived happily ever after, but change takes place over a period of time through practice, practice and practice. Alex had to keep reminding his mom not to share her heartaches with him. He requested that his dad spend some time with him. His father agreed and thus began a new phase in both of their lives. Jason and Alex agreed to talk on the phone frequently, getting to know one another as adults.

Alex's father was still emotionally unavailable, so Alex needed to continue receiving love from his male friends and mentors. He eventually accepted the fact that his father could not give him what he didn't experience himself. This realization created a peaceful state in his heart and soul. No longer did he look to Dad for the love he was unable to give. Alex saw his father for who he was and learned to be grateful for what he could give. Alex's love for his father was now one of gratitude and maturity.

Alex began dating. His attractions for women began to emerge after healing the homo-emotional/social wounds and fulfilling the unmet needs. After a year of dating several women, Alex met Christina. She was a very lovely and open woman. After some time, he shared about his past and his healing journey. She was very moved by his commitment to change, his perseverance, and his deep faith in God. Eventually they married and had three children. Now, Alex is a good father to his children and a better husband than his father was able to be. Of course, the road is not always easy, as shadows of the past reveal themselves. However, Alex and Christina have tools to use as they work through their respective issues. She, too, has done much healing work to restore her past. They continue to grow individually, as a couple and as a family.

Alex's therapy lasted almost three years. It took approximately one year for him to break his addictive cycle. Through that time period, he built a solid Support Network and learned many skills to gain a better sense of self. Through the passageway of his inner child, the wounds of his past emerged. Healing took place through many methods, as I have already described. Alex experienced his own gender identity as he removed the shields of detachment between himself and his father and brother. His needs were fulfilled through healthy male bonding. He learned more about women by being mentored by a generous woman. The Family Healing Session helped create an opening to establish new relationships with his father, mother and siblings. Alex continues to grow each day as a son of God, husband, father and powerful man in the world.

This is a very brief description of the Four Stages of resolving unwanted SSA. Once again, please read Chapters Four and Six in *Being Gay* for a more detailed explanation about the process of healing and various therapeutic techniques and tools. Also, read our *Clinician's Handbook: Assisting Our LGBTQ+ Loved Ones* (and watch the film series) for additional therapeutic modalities.

A THERAPIST'S GUIDE

Need for Healthy Touch in the Healing Process

I feel compelled to open this proverbial "can of worms," as most therapists are afraid to broach the subject of touch in the healing process. As the former client who struggled with unwanted SSA, experiencing healthy touch was a pre-requisite for my transformation and maturation into manhood. Having been sexually abused by my uncle when I was five, beaten by my older brother, and never touched, hugged or held by my dad, I was both touch abused and touch deprived. As a substitute, I had sex with men in a failed attempt to fill the empty hole in my soul. If only it had worked, but alas, it never did. Without the participation of three heterosexual male mentors, who offered me the gift of healthy touch, I never would have healed and become the man that I am today. As a therapist, I understand this important need for healthy touch for many of those who wish to resolve their unwanted SSA.

Please read Chapter Ten (pages 257 – 266) entitled "Touch: The Need for Bonding and Attachment" in *Being Gay*, and the section on "Touch" from my recent book *Healing Humanity: Time, Touch and Talk*. There I describe how we all need to experience healthy touch on a regular basis. Three scientists influenced me personally and professionally:

1) Ashley Montagu, Ph.D. (Princeton University), *Touching: The Human Significance of the Skin* (New York: William Morrow, 3rd edition, 1986).
2) Martha G. Welch, M.D. (Columbia University), *Holding Time* (New York: Simon & Shuster, 1988).
3) Tiffany Field, Ph.D. (University of Miami), where she is the Director of the Touch Research Institute.

There are more recent studies and wonderful books about our undeniable need for healthy touch, and the application of touch in the therapeutic setting and healing process.

It is very important to understand the significance of healthy touch in the healing process, as many men and women who experience unwanted SSA are touch deprived. Why have they been touch-deprived? Basically, there was a disruption in attachment between them and either their same-gender parent and/or same-gender peers. Often many of them were over-attached to their opposite-gender parent and/or opposite-gender peers. Therefore, in the process of reclaiming one's sense of true gender identity, there needs to be a resolution of this attachment need in healthy, same-gender, non-sexual relationships.

Touch will need to be administered with great compassion, sensitivity and understanding at the right times and by the right people. The ones to offer healthy touch must be secure in their sense of gender identity. The ideal candidates are happily married men and women. If the individual's parents are available, willing and emotionally/mentally healthy, they are the best candidates to administer this gift of healthy touch. If however they are unavailable, unwilling or unhealthy, then it is ill advised to have them be the bearers of touch for the man or woman in recovery.

In our *Clinician's Handbook: Assisting Our LGBTQ+ Loved Ones*, I discuss the application of healthy touch in the healing process by covering the following topics:

1) Development of healthy gender identity
2) Four stages of healing
3) Three stages in the mentoring relationship
4) Proper self-care: avoiding codependent relationships

Additionally, read the chapter on "Mentoring: Restoring Love" (pages 277–299) in *Being Gay*.

There are two distinct issues here:

1) Giving and receiving healthy touch in one's life
2) The use of healthy touch in the therapeutic setting

I am ***not*** advocating for the use of touch between the therapist and client. Most importantly the client needs to find healthy, heterosexual friends and mentors who may offer the gift of healthy touch. Having said this, I know it is extremely difficult for these men and women to find mentors who are willing to demonstrate healthy touch. I often suggest to clients, after they create a healthy relationship with either a friend or a mentor, to gently share about this issue, e.g., "While growing up, I never experienced being held, hugged or touched by my dad or any other male family member. I would be so grateful if you would be willing to give me a hug. I'm not interested in sex or anything like that, just a healthy hug between two friends." This is just an example. When any of my clients had created a close relationship with a friend and/or mentor, I suggested showing him/her the holding/healthy touch photos in *Being Gay*, page 288 (see the photos below). Additionally, I invited my client to bring his/her mentor(s) to a session so that I was able to demonstrate healthy touch and holding. This has worked beautifully, both in-person and via online video sessions.

And now the topic that dare not be mentioned: Is it appropriate, at any time, for the therapist to hold his client? Believe it or not, there are scientific studies which discuss the need and application of touch in the healing process between the therapist and client. Here are two such studies:

> *Use of physical touch in the "Talking Cure": A journey to the outskirts of psychotherapy*, Verena Bonitz, American Psychological Association, © 2008, Psychotherapy, Theory, Research, Practice, Training, Vol. 45, No. 3, 391-404. https://www.

scribd.com/document/48292116/Bonitz-2008-Use-of-Physical-touch-1#

Abstract

"The present literature review examines how physical touch has been used by therapists with their clients in traditional verbal psychotherapy. Attitudes and practices of therapists are presented in a historical context, starting with physicians' treatment of female hysteria in the 19th century, and concluding with current issues of debate. The use of touch in therapy has been highly controversial ever since Freud stated his principle of abstinence. This paper intends to give an overview of the various positions of influential therapists on the use of touch and their rationale for touching or not touching their clients, including the contextual factors that have shaped the use of touch over time. Furthermore, research findings pertinent to the use of touch in psychotherapy are included. The review concludes with practical recommendations concerning the use of touch in the contemporary therapeutic setting. (PsycINFO Database Record (c) 2010 APA, all rights reserved)."

> *Exploring the use of touch in the psychotherapeutic setting: A phenomenological review*, James E. Phelan, Psychotherapy Theory, Research, Practice, Training, American Psychological Association © 2009, Vol. 46, No. 1, 97-111. https://www.

PART I: BLUEPRINT FOR HEALING

academia.edu/33514359/Exploring_the_use_
of_touch_in_the_psychotherapeutic_setting_A_
phenomenological_review

Abstract

"This paper provides a synthesis of the literature concerning the duality of touch and talk between therapist and client in the psychotherapy setting. It discusses the ethical considerations, prohibitions, and attitudes about touch within the psychotherapeutic field. In addition, it looks at the client's perception of touch, types of touch, paradigms, rationales for the use of touch, religious and cultural considerations, the effects of touch, and research implications. Despite the reservations and lack of training around the use of touch in psychotherapy, there is a variety of literature to support its uses, benefits, effectiveness, and rationales, insomuch as there is a variety of literature about prohibitions, contraindications, and cautions of its use."

There are more scientific studies regarding the use of touch in the therapeutic setting. I am not advocating for this, merely bringing into the light what many therapists do and never share about with their colleagues. So, should and can you hold your clients? That is entirely up to you and your client. If you decide to do this:

1) Have your Informed Consent Agreement (contract with your client) clearly state how the use

of touch is expressly for a therapeutic purpose, and the client has the right to accept or reject this approach.

2) Set healthy boundaries and discuss about the obvious transference that will take place, i.e., you will become the dad he never had, you will become the first male he bonds with, the client may feel sexually aroused while being held, etc.

3) Have you yourself experienced healthy touch while growing up or during your own healing? One cannot give to another what one has not experienced and is not experiencing on a regular basis in the present.

It is imperative to discuss every aspect about the use of healthy touch if you choose to do this with a client.

In all honesty, I held my clients during the first fifteen years of my practice (since that time I have taught their mentors/friends how to provide this, either in-person or through online sessions). Healthy boundaries were discussed, and we always processed afterwards what the client experienced. My golden rule was, "First the crap, and then the lap!" Meaning, most often, first he needed to vent, express any hurtful, angry feelings (in constructive ways). Then, if he expressed a need, I would hold him, as I did for my three (now adult) children while they were growing up. It was imperative for me to always stay in the parental position, while the client was in the child position.

Only his needs were given attention. If I experienced any countertransference, I dealt with that afterwards either in my own processing time or with a supervisor or mentor. It is of the utmost importance for the therapist never to get his needs met from the client. This would parentify the client again, as he may have experienced taking care of his parent(s) in his family of origin.

In conclusion, this issue is greatly overlooked in the literature of resolving unwanted SSA. In my clinical practice, and training thousands of other therapists throughout the world, I always emphasize this important and overlooked issue. If we teach men and women, who experience unwanted SSA, how to find healthy touch in non-sexual relationships with those of the same gender, it will greatly reduce their amount of time in therapy and escalate the healing process.

Healthy touch demonstrated by Richard Cohen and his youngest son, Alfred.

PART II

Blueprint for Assisting Families and Friends with SSA Loved Ones: Twelve Principles for Change

Gay Children, Straight Parents: A Plan for Family Healing, Richard Cohen (Westmont, IL: InterVarsity Press, 2007; Bowie, MD: PATH Press, revised edition, 2016).

In addition to helping men and women resolve their unwanted SSA, I have assisted hundreds of parents in reconciling with their LGBTQ+ loved ones. In some cases, the parents were able to help their child come out of homosexuality, not through coercion but by setting love in order. Allow me to give a very brief overview of this twelve-step program as described in *Gay Children, Straight Parents: A Plan for Family Healing*.

Introduction

Many parents and family members are in shock when they first discover that their child or relative is gay, lesbian, bisexual, transgender, non-binary, etc. "What happened?" "Our son grew up in a loving, faith-based family." "Is this our fault? I know that we made mistakes, but really, did we cause this to happen?" "What can we do?"

Perhaps the parents are gripped with guilt, shame, anger, pain and so much more. Perhaps their dreams for grandchildren (from a heterosexual marriage) are dashed. Perhaps they judged their son or daughter when he or she "came out." All of these responses are normal. I always tell the parents, "You did not create your child's Same-Sex Attraction (SSA), or any identity of the LGBTQ+ community. This is always the result of many contributing factors—temperamental, environmental and/or familial. SSA is a bio-psycho-social phenomenon. It most often represents hurts in the heart that have not healed, and legitimate unmet love needs."

I further tell them, "Do not worry if you said all the wrong things when she/he came out. You may restore and improve the relationship with your SSA/LGBTQ+ loved one. Be assured that deep down inside, she/he is hungry for your love, acceptance and approval. Most likely it took many years for your loved one to 'come out.'"

Parents may fear that others will find out about their LGBTQ+ child, e.g., family members, friends and/or spiritual community members. You will need to help them manage their fears (exercises for this are included in the book). It is also your job to teach them that change ensues when healing occurs—when the wounds are addressed, and the unmet love needs fulfilled in healthy same-gender relationships, their child will experience the fullness of her or his gender identity, and heterosexual desires may ensue. Deep down your SSA daughter or son has felt, through most of her or his life, "I don't belong," "I don't fit in," and "I'm different" from the other girls or boys. SSA is about internalized thoughts and emotions of detachment from oneself and others. Therefore, it will take time to undo the years of thinking and feeling this way.

Next, I educate them about the socialization of the LGBTQ+ paradigm: "born gay and cannot change." As I described in Part I, I inform them about the Seven Stages of Coming Out: 1) Causes of SSA, 2) Same-sex attractions begin, 3) Conflict over SSA, 4) Need for belonging, 5) Indoctrination, 6) Identity acceptance as gay, lesbian, bisexual, transgender, non-binary, etc., and 7) Coming out process. Generally, the parents are the last to know. Why? Because they are the least important? No, it is because they are the *most* important. Their son or daughter was building a network of support among the gay-affirming community in case the parents rejected him or her and withdrew their love.

I instruct the parents to never insist that their child see a therapist to help them "change." Through years of indoctrination via online LGBTQ+ websites, social media, movies, etc., they were taught:

1) This type of therapy (pejoratively called "Conversion Therapy") leads to depression and potential suicide.
2) It does not work and creates more harm.
3) This concept of "change" is rejected by most mental health organizations.
4) Those who promote this therapy are homophobic and anti-gay.
5) Those who believe in this are ignorant of what science says, i.e., born gay and cannot change.

Therefore, the parents should never push their child to "change," or see a therapist for this purpose.

Overview of this program for parents, family members and friends with SSA loved ones:

1) Educate themselves about SSA.
2) Educate themselves about the homosexual movement.
3) They are now entering the world of their SSA loved one—feelings of guilt, shame, not belonging, being scared of how others will think and feel about them; all of these feelings and thoughts are what their SSA loved one experienced for many years.
4) Join with their SSA loved one—listen, learn and use good communication skills.

PART II: BLUEPRINT FOR ASSISTING FAMILIES AND FRIENDS

5) Establish trust, do things together, attend their meetings.
6) Seek professional help for themselves—therapy, seminars, family healing sessions.
7) Pray: you may read more about this in Step Three.

The goal of this 12-step treatment plan is to create intimacy and secure attachment between father-son and mother-daughter; to facilitate bonding with relatives and friends of the same gender; to set love in order, and to create healthy boundaries with the opposite-gender parent. Within this 12-step program are details about how parents and relatives may win back the heart of their SSA loved one.

Over the past 35 years in my clinical practice, 90% of the time, mothers are the ones that call our office if there is an SSA son, and fathers are the ones that call if there is an SSA daughter. Truly, 90% of the time this rings true. If a dad calls about his SSA son, I believe there might be a better prognosis for change and success. If a mother calls about her SSA daughter, this too may foreshadow hope for real change. And the most important change will be shifting the dynamics of the entire family system. More about this is explained in the 12-step plan.

Tell the parents, family members and friends NOT to constantly repeat their moral views about homosexuality. *Stating this just once is sufficient.* Part of SSA is oppositional behavior because of the defensive detachment with their same-gender parent and/or same-gender relatives and peers. This detachment resulted in a wounded heart and soul. Deep within anyone who experiences SSA or gender confusion, is a hurt and angry child. If the parents repeat their moral and religious views about homosexuality more than once, they will push their child further away and into the homosexual community. Parents must be wise, and offer unconditional love at all times.

By the way, do not use the term "homosexual lifestyle." Calling it a "style" is as offensive to them as suggesting they chose to experience SSA. "Are you living a heterosexual 'style' of life? It is not my 'style.' It is who I am!" I was taught this important nuance by a wonderful LGBTQ+ Bishop in Washington, D.C.

Here are the magic words for parents to share with their SSA child: "I love and accept you just the way you are." What? Cohen, are you crazy? No, I am not crazy. These words are specifically designed to help the child experience real love and genuine acceptance (I know that parents may need to go through a lot internally before being able to say this authentically and with love). "I love and accept you just the way you are." This is how God thinks about each one of us. He doesn't always agree with our choices and behaviors, and He never stops pouring out His unconditional love. Parents will now enter into a new realm of love.

Many parents have asked, "If I say this, won't she/he think that we approve of their behavior?" My response is, "It doesn't matter what she/he thinks. As long as you continue to demonstrate unconditional love, you are laying the groundwork for real change." "Yes, but what if my child asks, 'Does this mean that you've changed your mind? You now approve of me living a gay life?'" OK, listen carefully. The parent must SMILE while shaking his head back and forth saying, "No," which is quickly followed by the parent shaking his head up and down while saying, "And I love and accept you just the way you are!" Voila! Speaking the truth in love, unconditional love.

It's imperative to smile while saying "No," simultaneously shaking one's head back and forth; then quickly change to, "And I love and accept you just the way you are," while shaking one's head up and down. This is counterintuitive, but it works! In all my years of mentoring parents, this has proven true.

There is a big difference between Acceptance and Approval. I may accept someone unconditionally, while at the same time disapproving of their choices or behaviors. However, I keep my thoughts of disapproval to myself. This strategy was crafted through many years of trial and error, and it's tried, tested and true in its application with SSA loved ones.

You must warn the parents to never try and educate an LGBTQ+ loved one about the real science of SSA, that people aren't essentially born this way and that change is possible. My motto is:

A THERAPIST'S GUIDE

Win the heart, and the head will follow.

You cannot talk someone out of experiencing SSA. You cannot convince him or her this is "wrong," "unhealthy," "against religious truths," or "not based on real science." It will not work.

Win the heart, and the head will follow.

I will share many practical exercises how parents may demonstrate real love with their SSA child.

Getting married to someone of the opposite sex is *never* the solution for SSA. First, they must heal their own gender identity, then and only then can they be successful with someone of the opposite sex.

God will do the changing.
Ones' parents, relatives, and/or friends'
responsibility, is to love ceaselessly,
in all its forms.

It is imperative for the family members to take care of themselves, their relationship, and their other children. *This is a marathon, not a sprint.* They need to experience

God's love; take care of themselves and each other, and create a community of love. It may sound ridiculous, however, the child's SSA will ultimately become a blessing if the parents begin this healing journey. It will eventually transform them and their entire family. Money back guarantee!

Finally, here is the motto and theme of this strategic plan:

•••••••••••••••••••••••••••

This is a battle of love, and whoever loves the most and the longest wins!

•••••••••••••••••••••••••••

I ask the parents to keep this motto in a memo on their phones, somewhere they can see it several times per day, repeating it over and over again:

•••••••••••••••••••••••••••

This is a battle of love, and whoever loves the most and the longest wins!

•••••••••••••••••••••••••••

According to the research of LGBTQ+ therapists, long-term male SSA couples generally agree to have sex with other gay men outside of their relationship. With female SSA couples, there is often a high degree of emotional upheaval, and at times this upheaval may turn violent. If and when the child's relationship terminates, the parents will be the last one standing. They will be there to comfort their son or daughter after and/or through their vicissitudes of pain.

• •

This is a battle of love, and whoever loves the most and the longest wins!

• •

PART II: BLUEPRINT FOR ASSISTING FAMILIES AND FRIENDS

Syllabus for a Parents Support Group

I facilitated online Parents Support Groups for years. Here is the syllabus so that you may see how I led these groups, and the many homework assignments required of the parents. Research demonstrates that those who do homework assignments in therapy heal quicker. I tell the parents, *"It is imperative for you to change your perspective—from changing your child to changing yourself, your relationship with your partner (if still married), and the dynamics of your family system."*

Note: All group participants will need their own copy of *Gay Children, Straight Parents: A Plan for Family Healing* (GCSP).

Week 1: Introduction:

1. Introduce yourself, first names (5-7 minutes maximum per family, depending on how many couples/individuals are present):
2. Where do you live in the world?
3. Ages of your child or children?
4. A bit about your family situation and SSA child?
5. What you want to learn and gain from this class/support group?

- Review the entire syllabus and then email the participants The Feelings Wheel for them to practice (you may download The Feelings Wheel from

A THERAPIST'S GUIDE

our website: https://www.timetouchandtalk.com/time).

Homework:

1) Practice using The Feelings Wheel daily: share with your spouse two feeling words and what's behind your feelings.
2) Read the Introduction and Step One from *Gay Children, Straight Parents* (GCSP).
3) Do the exercise in Step One about sharing with your SSA child (dealing with your guilt and shame), both husband and wife. Do **not** do this exercise with your SSA child. This is for you to expunge the toxic guilt and shame from your soul. Do the exercise with your spouse or a trusted friend.

Week 2:

1. Two feeling words check-in (each participant).
2. Share about the homework: What did you learn from reading the Introduction and Step One? Let each person share succinctly, depending on the number of participants.
3. Did you do the exercise about sharing your guilt and shame regarding your SSA child? How was it for you? (Repeat the exercise as often as necessary.)
4. How are you taking care of yourself and the relationship with your spouse (if they are still married)?

5. Teach about the major points in the Introduction and Step One.

[As the facilitator, be mindful of those who talk a lot and those who do not share. Be sure to keep a balance between these two types. Ask the more quiet ones to share, and ask the more talkative ones to give opportunity for others to speak. Additionally, keep the balance between positive feedback and those who may tend to share only negative things.]

Homework:

1) Practice sharing two feeling words daily with your partner, and what's behind your feelings?
2) Read Steps Two and Three of GCSP.
3) Make a list of members of your Support Network. Begin to develop a Support Network if you don't have one. We will create an e-list of the parents in our group if you wish to share with and support each other.
4) Purchase *Ten Days to Self-Esteem* by David Burns and *Recovery of Your Inner Child* by Lucia Capacchione. Start to do the exercises in either one of these books. Share your homework with your spouse. Take your time, do one chapter every two weeks. These are not just books to read, but workbooks.

Week 3:

1. Two feeling words check-in (each participant).
2. Share about what you learned in Steps Two and Three of GCSP.
3. How is your homework coming along? Developing your Support Network?
4. Did you begin to do the exercises in *Recovery of Your Inner Child* (after finishing inner child exercises, begin doing *Ten Days to Self-Esteem*)? How was that for you?
5. Teach about the major points in Steps Two and Three (GCSP). Also, if time permits, teach about the Ten Causes of SSA.

Homework:

1) Practice sharing two feeling words daily with your partner, and what's behind your feelings?
2) Do the creative visualization exercise: email your three S-statements to me so that I may review them (see page 62 of GCSP for the details about the three Ss.)
3) Continue doing the exercises from the Inner Child or Ten Days books.
4) Read Step Four of GCSP.

Week 4:

1. Two feeling words check-in.
2. How is it going with using your visualizations (3-Ss)?
3. What did you learn in Step Four of GCSP?
4. How is it coming along with the exercises from the Inner Child and/or Ten Days book?
5. Review Step Four of GCSP as necessary.

Homework:

1) Practice sharing two feeling words daily with your partner, and what's behind your feelings?
2) Make a list of what you believe contributed to your child's SSA? (GCSP pp. 70-75)
   [Each parent does this independently and then they share their lists with each other. Finally, they make a combined list of why they believe their child experiences SSA.]
3) Begin to create a treatment plan for your child: based on their wounds that have not healed and unmet love needs (examples of the Treatment Plans are at the back of GCSP).
4) Visit 4 websites: 2 pro-LGBTQ+ / 2 pro-healing. For example:

Pro-LGBTQ+ websites include:

- https://www.hrc.org
- https://www.glsen.org

Pro-healing websites include:

- https://www.pathinfo.org
- https://www.therapeuticchoice.com.

5) Continue doing the exercises from the Inner Child or Ten Days books.

Week 5:

1. Two feeling words check-in.
2. Share about your homework: creating the evaluations and starting to make your treatment plans.
3. What did you learn from viewing the LGBTQ+ websites, and the healing websites?
4. What issues have come to your attention that you need to personally address?
5. How are the exercises coming along from the Inner Child or Ten Days books?

Homework:

1) Practice sharing two feeling words daily with your partner, and what's behind your feelings?
2) Continue working on your treatment plan for your SSA child.
3) Make a schedule of activities; make goals SMART: Simple, Measurable, Achievable, Realistic, Timely.
4) Read Step Five of GCSP.

Week 6:

1. Two feeling words check-in.
2. What did you learn from reading Step 5 of GCSP or anything else during the week?
3. How is it going with creating your treatment plan?
4. How is it going with the Inner Child or Ten Days exercises?
5. Review Step Five from GCSP, Communication Skills: sharing and listening.

Homework:

1) Practice sharing two feeling words daily with your partner, and what's behind your feelings?
2) Practice effective listening and sharing skills with your spouse, child/children, friends, work colleagues. Practice using the communication skills a minimum of 3 times per week.
3) Continue working on steps from your treatment plan. Celebrate each victory!
4) Read Step Six of GCSP.

Week 7:

1. Two feeling words check-in.
2. How is it going with the communication skills for effective sharing and listening?
3. What did you learn from Step Six in GCSP?
4. Discuss Step Six of GCSP and the exercises.
5. How it's going with your treatment plan?

Homework:

1) Practice sharing two feeling words daily with your partner, and what's behind your feelings?
2) Write Affirmations for your child (each parent does this individually). Email them to me to check.
3) Write a Letter to your child expressing regrets and asking forgiveness (each parent writes their own letter)—not in the context of SSA or gender confusion. Do not share this with you child (yet).
4) Continue exercises in the Inner Child or Ten Days book.

Week 8:

1. Two feeling words check-in.
2. How is it going with developing your Affirmations and writing the Letter?
3. How's it going with the Inner Child or Ten Days books?

Homework:

1) Practice sharing two feeling words daily with your partner, and what's behind your feelings?
2) Watch movies, e.g., "Man of the House" (old version with Chevy Chase and Farrah Fawcett) and "Life as a House."
3) Same-gender parent joins with the child in an activity of their child's choice and will share about it in the next class.

4) Read Step Seven from GCSP and define your child's love language and interests.

Week 9:

1. Two feeling words check-in.
2. Share something that was challenging or helpful.
3. What did you learn from Step Seven of GCSP?
4. Each parent shares how it is going—changing their family system/dynamics.

Homework:

1) Practice sharing two feeling words daily with your partner, and what's behind your feelings?
2) Read Steps Eight and Nine in GCSP.
3) Continue working on the Treatment Plan and doing the exercises from the book.
4) Continue exercises from the Inner Child or Ten Days books.

Week 10:

1. Check-in with two feeling words.
2. Share something that was challenging or helpful, and what you learned from Steps Eight and Nine of GCSP.
3. How are the exercises coming along from the Inner Child or Ten Days books?

4. Is the opposite-gender parent backing up and supporting the same-gender parent in bonding with his/her child?
   5. How is the same-gender parent doing in getting closer to the SSA child?

Homework:
   1) Practice sharing two feeling words daily with your partner, and what's behind your feelings?
   2) Read Steps Ten, Eleven, and Twelve in GCSP.
   3) Continue doing the exercises from GCSP.
   4) Continue doing the exercises from Inner Child and Ten Days books.

Week 11:

   1. Two feeling words check-in.
   2. Share something that was challenging or helpful.
   3. What did you learn from Steps Ten – Twelve in GCSP?
   4. How are the Inner Child or Ten Days exercises going?
   5. Teach from Steps Ten, Eleven and Twelve in GCSP.

Homework:
   1) Practice sharing two feeling words daily with your partner, and what's behind your feelings?
   2) Finish writing your Treatment Plans for Family Healing—Short Term & Long Term Goals (examples at the end of GCSP).

3) Make a list of people who can love your child: particularly same-gender siblings, relatives, friends and members of your spiritual community.

4) If you found the book helpful, please go to Amazon and write a positive book review of *Gay Children, Straight Parents: A Plan for Family Healing*. Many thanks☺

Week 12:

1. Two feeling words check-in.
2. Review your Treatment Plans (based on causes and needs—examples at the back of the GCSP book).
3. What are the most important things you have learned from the book and your journey this far?
4. Where do you go from here?

Be sure to have the parents share something positive during each session. It is easy for them to just express negative things. Therefore, have at least one or a few parents share small victories each class. This will hopefully inspire the others. Finally, you may organize a Parents Group over a much longer duration of time. As you just read, this was a very intense 12-week course. It could easily be a 20-week Parents Group. It's entirely up to you. Additionally, you may restart the group and they may begin it all over again. There is so much to learn and implement in this book/program.

A THERAPIST'S GUIDE

Summary of the Key Points from *Gay Children, Straight Parents:*

**Gay Children, Straight Parents:
A Plan for Family Healing**
Richard Cohen, M.A., Bowie, MD: PATH Press, 2016

Section One: Personal Healing

Step One:	Take Care of Yourself
Step Two:	Do Your Own Work
Step Three:	Experience God's Love

Section Two: Relational Healing

Step Four:	Investigate the Causes of SSA
Step Five:	Utilize Effective Communication Skills
Step Six:	Make Things Right between You and Your SSA Child
Step Seven:	Discover Your Child's Love Language and Participate in Their Interests
Step Eight:	Same-Gender Parent: Display Appropriate Physical Affection
Step Nine:	Opposite-Gender Parent: Take Two Steps Back

Section Three: Community Healing

Step Ten:	Create a Warm and Welcoming Environment in Your Home, Place of Worship and Community
Step Eleven:	Boyfriends, Girlfriends, Ceremonies and Sleepovers
Step Twelve:	Find Mentors and Mentor Others

© Richard Cohen, M.A., 2023

PART II: BLUEPRINT FOR ASSISTING FAMILIES AND FRIENDS

Two stories from parents who participated in our classes: **A Daughter's Homecoming,** *Gay Children, Straight Parents,* 2016, pp 132–136.

We found out about Sarah's SSA when she was nineteen years old, but didn't discuss it much after that. When she went to college, Sarah told us that she was having an affair with another girl in her youth group from the time she was fourteen. We responded negatively, thinking that homosexuality was worse than murder. We also believed that homosexuality was a choice. We thought she had chosen this herself.

Instead of compassion and sympathy, we responded in judgment. We told her, "You'll go to hell. This is sinful behavior." We had various arguments after that. She moved out and closer to the gay community downtown. She felt much better with them. There she was accepted.

We spent four years in that situation. We helped her out financially, but were at odds about everything else. There was no connection. She revealed to us later that she just wanted us to drive down there, especially mom, and pick her up and take her home. She told us that she had gone through the most brutal experiences of her life while living in the gay community. She said, "Mom and Dad, you threw me to the wolves!" We know that she hasn't told us everything, yet. She felt abandoned and left alone by the two people she loved and needed the most. She even contemplated suicide but didn't because she thought it would hurt us too deeply!

She was truly a child looking for love in all the wrong places because we didn't understand her in the ways that she needed at the time. We didn't love her as God loved her. We told her how we wanted her to be and how we needed her to conform to our demands. And it sent her straight into the arms of the sad gay world. We would be friendly one minute, then get angry the next and say things like, "Why are you living this horrible lifestyle?" We were critical of her and her friends and never socialized with them.

Several years ago, we were going to buy a house. The Spirit of God moved us to ask her if she wanted to live with us. She said she would if her girlfriend could live there too. Somehow we agreed. That was the beginning of reestablishing our relationship. But it lacked relational substance. We were still locked into the mindset that this was rebellious and chosen behavior. This produced anger and judgement, and caused us not to connect in the ways that she needed. We continued to neglect her essential needs for love.

Our church was very judgmental about homosexuality. We didn't feel comfortable to speak with anyone about this, so we ended up leaving. We felt alone, in pain and anguish. We quit going to church and tried desperately to find a place where we belonged.

A big break came when her girlfriend charged our credit card for thousands of dollars! Our daughter had the strength to throw her out of the house. We asked Sarah to see a counselor who was a friend of ours from church. She finally agreed to see him once and then began having regular sessions.

In late 2004, we said we must do something because we were in deep despair. I (Dad) went to my office one Saturday morning. I found in my desk drawer, among a group of papers, a letter to the editor I had kept for years that mentioned homosexuality. I had this piece of paper for so long it had turned brown! I believe this was divine intervention. In that article it mentioned PFLAG and PFOX. I eventually went to the PFOX website and spoke with the director. She told me about Richard Cohen. That was the beginning of our enlightenment.

Before Christmas of that year, we were going around in circles and getting nowhere. It was hurting our marriage. Our hearts had darkened until we met Richard. Then we participated in the Parents Class and attended one of Richard's Healing Seminars. The suffering and pain of the SSA strugglers at the seminar opened our eyes. We saw them crying and realized that our daughter felt the same way!

During the past eight months, we have progressed more than in the last six years. Last night, our daughter called saying, "I feel so much pain. Can I come over and share with you?" This would never have happened before. The turning point was realizing the truth about homosexuality. We finally understood that our daughter never chose to have same-sex attraction. We came to realize that SSA resulted from many of her life experiences and perceptions about events.

The truth lifted the veil of ignorance from our minds and allowed our hearts to love our daughter the way that she needed. The truth has set us free. Sarah recently said, "I haven't felt your love in six years. I feel closer to you now than ever before."

When we understood that she wasn't born this way and did not choose to have SSA, we were able to move from anger and judgment to compassion and love. This was the greatest lesson we learned in the parents classes and by attending Richard's healing seminar. There we witnessed the wounded hearts of so many men and women who struggle with SSA. We gained such a greater appreciation for our daughter.

Author's Note: Please read more of their story in *Gay Children, Straight Parents* (pages 132–136). Today, Sarah has been married to her husband for 14 years and they have three beautiful children. Their family is blossoming.

PART II: BLUEPRINT FOR ASSISTING FAMILIES AND FRIENDS

One Couple's Journey, *Gay Children, Straight Parents*, 2016, pp 161–165.

My wife and I are Lutheran pastors. We attended a presentation that Richard made two weeks after our son told us, with much anguish and many tears, that he was attracted to the same sex. Although we believed that people were born that way, we did not want it to be so for him, because of the potential persecution and agony that he would undoubtedly endure in living out his inborn sexuality. But we never admitted to either one of our children that we had not been able to reconcile our belief with the Scriptures.

We went to hear Richard talk about understanding and healing homosexuality. We sat near the back so we could leave "if things got too weird." His impassioned testimonial about his thirty-year struggle with unwanted SSA touched our hearts and minds on a level never before experienced. Though we initially squirmed when he said, "No one is born with SSA, and people can change," this made sense of a lot of what we had experienced as a family while raising our son and daughter. As we left the hall, we were speechless.

We purchased *Being Gay: Nature, Nurture or Both?* and that night we went home and haltingly shared this radical new learning with our son. He was furious at our interest in this approach and extremely angry that we would even consider a new direction, but thankfully, he was willing to listen.

My wife and I read the book and found our family's reality described on most of its pages. How blind we had been! We had all wholeheartedly bought into the "born that way and can't change" myth. We realized, in fact, that this myth had permeated our seminary education and theological underpinnings. These new ideas challenged that myth. We also discovered a loving truth that accurately makes sense of the Scriptures. We knew that God was indeed a God of love and possibility, and not a God of ignorance or avoidance. We had avoided facing the truth that we could not reconcile with the Scriptures, but we also knew that love was the answer and not prideful judgment or shame. We had been uncomfortable with particular groups, churches and denominations that had called homosexuality a sin and said that it could be "prayed away." We knew that wasn't quite right either.

Although our son was very angry that we had done a 180, he was willing to read the book, and we could tell that he was finding meaning in some of the things that he was reading. Of the ten different potential variables mentioned in the book that cause SSA, we realized that we could relate to eight of them. We decided to proceed to the Washington, D.C., area for a Family Healing Session with Richard. We were so grateful that our son was willing to attend.

It was one of the most incredible experiences in our lives. Though we have always cared for each other with a fierce love, we realized through family therapy that the dynamics of our relationship as husband and wife and pastor and pastor had profoundly affected our children. In particular, it had contributed to our son's same-sex attraction. Furthermore, some of our wounds and childhood needs were excavated, and we began to see how these influenced our son's detachment from me and overattachment to his mother.

I began to come to terms with the fact that I had a distant relationship with my father. Because of that, I tend to remain at a distance or emotionally unavailable. That was my preferred method of coping as a child and later as an adult. My wife realized that she had come from a long line of matriarchs and that, in some cases, men were subtly emasculated. She had also experienced abandonment and rejection as a child, which led her to be a needy adult. She realized that she had inadvertently expected our son to take care of some of those needs. Family therapy exposed some of our blind spots and changed our lives in ways we never before imagined.

Although it was difficult at first, my wife took a backseat with regard to our family. At times she would be silent at the table and that allowed my son and me to converse in a way that we had not done before. As for me, I began to concentrate on being emotionally present. I practiced active listening and tried not to react, but rather paraphrase and respond with questions. *I realized that it was more important for me to be in relationship with him than to be right all the time.*

My own heart and self-care have been of foremost importance in the healing process. I was parented in unhealthy ways while growing up. Now I am getting in touch with my own inner child, and he is teaching me important lessons. I am learning to more fully celebrate the process of becoming the man that God created me to be. My wife is keenly aware of becoming the woman that God created her to be as well. We realized that our son's bravado in sharing his same-sex attraction was the release our family needed to begin the process toward healing and wholeness.

We finally got real with each other, and this allowed our son to begin to express his childhood wounds and unmet needs. He began to share his hell with us. He told us what it was like to sustain peer rejection and criticism. We knew he had a sensitive spirit and that both of our children were confused about male and female gender roles within the family. My wife and I are now taking responsibility for our past failures and our family is healing.

As part of our family treatment plan, I held my son several times a week. Most often, he just sat there, not wanting to be in my presence or arms. But I determined to win him back! In all honesty, it was exhausting. And there were many setbacks along the way. After one year of doing this, he found a boyfriend. So I thought, this isn't working. And I quit holding my son.

After one week he came to me and said, "Dad, I feel so hurt that you gave up on me and stopped the holding."

I was shocked. I was humbled. And I determined not to quit this time, no matter what. And so we resumed our weekly holding sessions. Even though he still had a boyfriend, I fought hard to win him back. In time, that relationship did fall apart.

Our son graduated high school and went on to train with a professional theatrical company. He was steeped in the "gay" world but extremely unhappy. And then a miracle occurred. He met a wonderful group of men and women from a church that surrounded him with incredible love and affirmation. They invited him to move into a house with other youth group members. And so he did. More and more, while receiving the same-gender peer affirmation and attention he had never experienced in his life, we saw the walls around his heart melting day-by-day. Our son was coming alive; in fact he was blossoming and his faith rekindled for the first time in years.

Now he is determined to heal from his SSA. He himself requested another Family Healing Session to resolve the remaining issues he has with us and within himself. Recently he came home and has been sharing his newfound faith and freedom with his close friends. He even stood before the church congregation and shared his testimony of transformation. This new reality is a blessing beyond measure.

We are still dealing with our feelings of anger over the myth and how it ruins so many lives and robs so many people of their true personhood. We are grateful that we can harness some of that anger and channel it toward helping other people realize that *change is possible*. My wife and I are coming to terms with our new learning and reflecting on the way that the myth affected our family, our theological education, and our church family. We have hope. Our family is now experiencing newfound joy, healing and wholeness. Thank God.

Author's Note: What a remarkable story of changing the family culture, and taking responsibility for each family member's personal healing. Now their son has been married to a beautiful woman for eight years, and they have two gorgeous children. Dreams do come true!

Conclusion to GCSP

1. SSA has nothing to do with sex; it's a gender identity issue.
2. Parents write a personalized treatment plan and put it into action day-by-day.
3. Feel and be real in order to heal. Lead by example: Heal yourself.
4. Succeed small rather than fail big; take one step at a time. Celebrate each victory.
5. Whoever loves the most and the longest wins!

I know that I did not specifically address the transgender, non-binary, and other LGBTQ+ identities. I tell the parents to utilize the same principles from this book. Tell the parents: "Do not, do not, do not try to talk your child out of identifying as transgender or non-binary. It will not work." They must be unconditionally loving and utilize all the exercises from this book.

OK, here is my truth, and I don't mean to disappoint anyone. Over the past 35 years working with parents who have SSA and/or LGBTQ+ identified loved ones, the percentage of those who achieve the goal of helping their children come out straight or revert to their innate gender identity is very low. Why? Most parents want their kids to change without working to change themselves, their dysfunctional relationship(s), and the family dynamics. Has anyone been successful in changing his or her spouse or partner? Of course not. The only person we can change is ourself, and that's a lifelong odyssey. The good news is that parents who work on themselves, become closer as a couple, and change the family dynamics succeed. That's the formula for positive results. Once again, SSA is not the issue—it is a mask for a hurting heart and unmet love needs.

As you have seen, *Gay Children, Straight Parents* is a book filled with exercises and homework assignments. As a therapist, we lead by example. We must continuously work on ourselves to heal our own issues, improve our marriages (if we are married), and lovingly care for our children. Marriage and parenting are the most difficult jobs on earth. If we are not taking care of ourselves and our relationships, we have no business being in the helping profession!

Conclusion

Once again, for a more in-depth analysis of assisting those who experience unwanted SSA and their loved ones, please read:

1. *Being Gay: Nature, Nurture or Both?*
2. *Gay Children, Straight Parents: A Plan for Family Healing*
3. *Understanding Our LGBTQ+ Loved Ones*
4. *Clinician's Handbook: Assisting Our LGBTQ+ Loved Ones*

I would like to thank Dr. Jospeh Nicolosi Sr. for his pioneering work in this field of understanding the deeper meaning behind Same-Sex Attraction and application to the therapeutic process. His books helped in my personal and professional development. Please visit his website for more information: https://www.josephnicolosi.com. There are many other therapists who pioneered this field. My heartfelt thanks goes to all of them.

When I was a senior at Lower Merion High School in a suburb of Philadelphia, I did my final English term paper on male homosexuality. That was in 1970, and one dared not mention such a topic publicly. Well, I never allowed any social norms to stop me from pursuing the truth. Since I was young, I sought for a more profound understanding about the meaning of life. This was paramount to my existence. Additionally, finding books to help me understand my homosexual desires was of the utmost importance for my survival.

As a high school senior, I had the opportunity to audition as a piano major for the Eastman School of Music at the University of Rochester. While there, in some back alleys, down a dimly lit street, I found a gay bookstore. Nervously I entered, keeping my head down. I found and purchased one book that piqued my curiosity: Dr. Irving Bieber's *Homosexuality: A Psychoanalytic Study* published in 1962. It was a revelation! Someone spoke truth into my soul about the etiology of homosexual desires and the possibility for change.

I found several other titles and wrote a 26-page typed term paper on the origins and treatment of ego-dystonic homosexual feelings. I don't recall if I outed myself in the paper. All I can remember is that my teacher was surprised, delighted, and rewarded me with an "A+." Frankly I didn't care about the grade. I was writing this paper for myself, to help explain what I had been feeling for so many years.

CONCLUSION

I asked my parents for help, to see a psychiatrist because of my unwanted homosexual feelings. Remember this was 1970, and the subject was taboo. Saying the word "homosexual" out loud was a big "No, No." Well, that never stopped me. Somehow, I had enough self-respect and inner turmoil to ask for what I needed; again, all part of my endless pursuit of truth. To my parents' credit, they didn't overreact. My father tried to ignore the subject. My mother said, to my chagrin, "I always knew it!"

The first psychiatrist I saw, while still in high school, was Dr. Dryer. It was a total disaster. I doubt he had any understanding about the origins and treatment of unwanted SSA. So I quit. Several months later I was off to Boston University, where I began my studies as a piano major. We found another psychiatrist who would try and help me. For the next three years, I had two sessions per week with Dr. Julius Silberger. It was pure torture, so much pain and very little gain. He had me lay down on the sofa, in the traditional Freudian manner, and share whatever came to my heart and mind. Mostly he said, "I see," "Ah ha," "I understand." That was generally the depth and breadth of his responses, when he wasn't asking leading questions. It was psychic-numbing agony. Later I would come to understand that this type of therapeutic approach is contraindicated, as an intrinsic part of SSA is detachment. Traditional Freudian psychoanalysis reinforces the attachment strain and keeps the client in detachment mode.

A THERAPIST'S GUIDE

In my freshman year of college, I had a few boyfriends and then a male partner, Kurt, for the next three years. With all of my heart I tried to make our relationship work. Kurt and I played a cat-and-mouse game. I would pursue, he would often run away. We were two very tortured souls trying to figure this out. If only it had worked. If only, but it was obviously not meant to be.

Kurt and I parted ways in 1974. Having met a religious group that helped me in the pursuit of truth, I terminated our same-sex relationship, believing that this was not compatible with God's Word. For the next nine years I was celibate. During this time I met my wife-to-be, Jae Sook, who hails from South Korea. Being the honest soul that I was and am, I told her about my homosexual past. At least that is what I believed it to be was since I hadn't acted upon those desires for almost a decade. She was compassionate in her response. I felt relieved and grateful.

We married in 1980. At first it felt so romantic and lovely. Then the monster emerged, and that monster was me! I became so angry and controlling toward my wife. It was as if my father had possessed me. Shocked, horrified and angry, I went back into therapy. Oh yes, and my homosexual feelings re-emerged in living color. I was furious with God. "Why didn't you take these desires away? I did everything you asked of me. I was the perfect Christian man." I beat my fists on the floor, on my chest, and up to heaven. "Why? Why? Why?" Of course, during those nine years of celibacy I had intermittent same-sex desires, however, I was told to simply ignore and suppress those feelings, which I did.

We lived in New York City at that time. I was an artist manager organizing tours for classical musicians and ballet companies from the U.S.A. and Europe all over Asia: Japan, Korea, Taiwan, Singapore, Malaysia, China and the Philippines. I was very successful in my work, but my home life was miserable. To pay for therapy, I worked a second job as a waiter in a Japanese restaurant near the United Nations. Daytime I was an artist manager (touring with the artists or dancers throughout Asia often six times a year), and several nights a week I was waiting tables at the restaurant.

From May 1983, Dr. Robert Kronemeyer was my therapist. He was the author of *Overcoming Homosexuality* (1980). Slowly he helped me discover the origins of my unwanted SSA. He had trained with Dr. Alexander Lowen and Dr. Wilhelm Reich, founders of Bioenergetics. Through a variety of therapeutic modalities, he guided me back to the past where I shockingly discovered child sexual abuse by my uncle (Dr. Kronemeyer never insinuated that I had been abused; those memories emerged on their own). I raged, I screamed, I pounded, and I began this painful quest to uncover and discover the wounded child within.

It's exhausting to even remember those days: working two jobs, being a husband to my wife, taking care of our two young children, and going through the dark nights of my soul in therapy. Rather than resolve my unwanted

SSA, those desires returned with a vengeance. You see, my therapist did not help me develop a strong Support Network. People in my church, and other churches that I visited, did not understand about this phenomenon of homosexuality. I was on the outside looking in, and no one was opening the door.

I announced to my wife and therapist, "I need to be held by a man. I need to grieve and heal in the arms of a man; a healthy heterosexual man who is secure in his own gender identity and masculinity. I sought help from different religious groups, support groups, and social settings. No one, and I mean not one man was willing to hold this hungry soul. I don't want or need sex. I just require healthy touch from a man. So, I will seek some solace in the arms of a gay man." And that is what I did. Remember, we were living in New York City at that time, which is one of the gay capitals of the U.S.A. Into the sad gay world I went, looking for healthy touch, knowing that I would have to compromise my values and beliefs to experience some touch and holding.

You will have to wait several more years for me to share additional details of what I experienced during those tumultuous years. I kept journals for the next twenty years of my journey, both through healing unwanted SSA, and then becoming a therapist helping others from 1989 on. My personal breakthrough occurred in February 1987, and off to Seattle, Washington we went, where I attended graduate school for counseling psychology and started my practice as a psychotherapist. In summary, the two main salient points that I wish to convey are these:

First, do not, do not, do *not* engage in psychodynamic therapy (Stages Three and Four of the healing process) before the client is emotionally and mentally stable, and has a strong Support Network. Without him or her experiencing a healthy internal ego-structure, and having a supportive environment, he or she will seek love in all the wrong places, betraying his or her own sense of integrity.

Second, this is a developmental, gender identity issue. Sex will never solve anyone's SSA, because, once again, the desires are those of a child in need of healthy bonding and secure attachment with members of the same gender. SSA men must heal with OSA men, and SSA women must heal with OSA women. That's a formula for continued growth into manhood or womanhood.

So you see, I know this issue from the inside out. I can talk the talk because I have walked the walk, and helped so many heal and fulfill their heterosexual dreams. Dreams do come true. Please help these sensitive souls on the journey to reclaim their true gender identity.

Please allow me to succinctly repeat several of the **Lessons Learned** over the past thirty-five years in my clinical practice:

1 – SSA is not about sex. Your client may come to you saying, "I don't want to be gay. I don't want to live a gay life. Please help me resolve these feelings and be strictly heterosexual." First, give him or her hope that change *is* possible. Next, you need to reframe their concept of being "gay" and being "heterosexual." They want to be rid of these unwanted feelings. However, these feelings are a message from their soul, trying to get their attention. SSA is not bad. SSA is not evil. SSA is not a curse from God or the Devil. SSA is the psyche's attempt to communicate that something is hurting inside, needs attention, resolution, and the right kinds of love.

It took years to develop SSA, therefore it will take time to resolve the issues that created those desires. Generally, the process of healing takes 1½ to 3 years. The amount of time it takes to resolve unwanted SSA is dependent upon *severity, sincerity and support:* 1) the severity of wounding experienced in childhood/adolescence, 2) the effort that he/she is willing to invest in the healing process, and 3) the number of men/women in his or her Support Network. Without healthy, heterosexual men, he will not be able to grow into the fullness of his masculinity, and may therefore continuously sexualize normal needs for bonding. She too needs healthy, heterosexual women to surround her with lots of positive, feminine non-sexual love and attention.

2 – Assure them that they don't need to "get rid" of SSA. When they resolve the hurts of their past, the quiet or obvious traumas that occurred in early childhood and/or adolescence, and experience healthy love from those of their same gender, SSA will naturally diminish, and opposite-sex attractions will ensue. We are all biologically designed as heterosexuals, as men and women fit perfectly together. Two men or two women do not.

3 – If there is a dual diagnosis, or comorbidity, first you or another specialist must help the client resolve the other issue(s), i.e., alcohol addiction, porn and masturbation addiction, substance abuse, etc. Unless they begin to resolve their addiction(s), he or she will continuously revert to this pattern of behavior when experiencing stress or pain, and delay any possibility of healing. If the client is unable or unwilling to deal with his or her addiction(s), or other diagnosis, it is unprofessional of you to attempt to assist him or her.

4 – As Dr. Dean Byrd said, "Be more than a therapist, and less than a parent." You are their cheerleader. You must be the light bringer—they will know the truth (about themselves), and the truth will eventually set them free. Encourage them to never, ever give up. Keep instilling hope in him. Keep her on the path. Follow the four-stages of healing. Just "be there" for them when they feel hopeless and discouraged. Be their biggest cheerleader. Instill hope for their outcome, to fulfill their dreams. "You can do it. I believe in you. I will be by your side. Never give up!" More than a therapist, less than a parent.

5 – Time alone does not heal wounds; it only buries them deeper. We need to help the client trace and face what happened, grieve the losses of his or her past, and experience new and healthy love from those capable of giving it.

6 – The wounds experienced in hurtful relationships must be healed in healthy relationships. We cannot heal on our own because all issues are relational. Grieving alone into one's pillow at night will not do it. That kind of grief will become cyclical. Real love must be experienced in healthy relationships in order to heal old wounds. We need to share our truth, feel accepted, build trust, and then experience real love. Remember, there are no quick fixes in the matters of the heart. Additionally, as the therapist or coach, you must, must, must help the client build a strong Support Network. He needs healthy OSA men to be his friends and mentors. She needs the same, with OSA women. Learn more about building the Support Network in *Being Gay*, Chapters Four and Six.

7 – Please let your client know that when stressed or under duress, their old habits may emerge as a coping mechanism. They have not gone backwards or regressed if he or she once again experiences SSA. It is merely the repetition of an old neurological pattern. The key is to understand that it is not about the old habit (unwanted SSA), it is about dealing with the present situation and circumstances in healthy and effective ways. As soon as she or he takes good care of herself/himself, or perhaps remembers moments of being loved, then the vestiges of any past unhealthy patterns will fade away and she or he will feel much better. Additionally, if someone experienced sexual abuse or other forms of same-sex activity at a young age, the brain's neural-pathways were formatted to experience SSA. Therefore, again, under stress a fallback response may be same-sex attraction. It only means that the remnants of the old, unhealthy wiring are being fired up due to stress. One should breathe, relax, get in touch with one's soul, and listen to what it is trying to communicate. It is never about SSA (or sex), it is about proper self-care and learning to love and be loved.

8 – SSA is a gift to help men and women heal, grow, and become who they are truly meant to be. Teach them that SSA is actually their best friend. Help him or her to embrace the issue, listen to it, learn from it, and become a good steward of his/her soul. In the process of growth, he/she will become a more loving man/woman. Then, they will bless others because they have journeyed through their own personal hell and returned as more healthy people, capable of loving and offering their gifts to others.

9 – "You are not gay." "You are not a homosexual." "You are not bisexual." "You are not non-binary." "You are not transgender." "You are either a precious Son or Daughter of God (and for those having no particular spiritual beliefs: "You are either a man or woman"). That is your true identity." This is so important to convey to your client at the outset of therapy. "Gay," "Homosexual," "Bisexual," "Non-binary," "Transgender" are all man-made terms. They are inaccurate labels. In cultures today, these terms are used as nouns, putting people in boxes. However, SSA is an adjective, describing someone's thoughts, feelings and desires.

10 – You must be real and feel in order to heal. Stage One is behavioral therapy. Stage Two is cognitive therapy. Stages Three and Four are psychodynamic therapy. Of course, throughout the four stages of recovery, clients are learning to get in touch with their inner world and their deeper feelings. If a therapist merely engages in "talk therapy" without helping the client become more in tune and touch with his or her heart, real and lasting change will not occur.

I hope this book will help you as you help others. It is my wish that the truth about homosexuality will one day be known by all. In the meantime, please be agents of change in your world: helping one life at a time. We will change history together!

Resources

Patrick Carnes, *Out of the Shadows: Understanding Sexual Addiction*, Center City, MN: Hazelden Publishing, 3rd Edition, 2010.

Richard Cohen, *Being Gay: Nature, Nurture or Both?*, Bowie, MD: PATH Press, 2020.

Richard Cohen, *Clinician's Handbook: Assisting Our LGBTQ+ Loved Ones*, Bowie, MD: PATH Press, 2008, revised edition 2023.

Richard Cohen, *Gay Children, Straight Parents: A Plan for Family Healing*, Westmont, IL: InterVarsity Press, 2007, revised edition, PATH Press, Bowie, MD, 2016.

Richard Cohen, M. Waseem, Illustrator, *Rich's Home*, Bowie, MD: PATH Press, 2022.

Richard Cohen, *Understanding Our LGBTQ+ Loved Ones*, Bowie, MD: PATH Press, 2022.

Norman Doidge, *The Brain that Changes Itself: Stories of Personal Triumph from the Frontiers of Brain Science*, New York: Penguin Books, 2007.

Janelle Hallman, *The Heart of Female Same-Sex Attraction*, Westmont, IL: InterVarsity Press, 2008.

Elizabeth R. Moberly, *Homosexuality: A New Christian Ethic*, Cambridge, UK: Lutterworth Press, revised edition 2006.

Joseph Nicolosi Sr., *Reparative Therapy of Male Homosexuality: A New Clinical Approach*, Northvale, NJ: Jason Aronson, Inc, 1991, Liberal Mind Publishers, 2020.

Joseph Nicolosi Sr., *A Parent's Guide to Preventing Homosexuality*, Liberal Mind Publishers, revised edition, 2017.

Joseph Nicolosi Sr., *Shame and Attachment Loss: The Practical Work Of Reparative Therapy*, Westmont, IL: InterVarsity Press, 2009, Liberal Mind Publishers, 2016.

James Phelan, *Successful Outcomes of Sexual Orientation Change Efforts*, Phelan Consultants LLC, 2014.

Jay Stringer, *Unwanted: How Sexual Brokenness Reveals Our Way to Healing*, Jay Stringer, Carol Stream, IL: NavPress, Tyndale House Publishers, Inc., 2018.

Mark Woylnn, *It Didn't Start With You: How Inherited Family Trauma Shapes Who We Are and How to End the Cycle*, New York: Penguin Books, 2017.

Organizations

Therapeutic / Healing Organizations

- Alliance for Therapeutic Choice and Scientific Integrity (Professional Therapists)
  www.therapeuticchoice.com
- Brothers Road
  https://www.brothersroad.org
  On-line support groups for men / JIM weekend experience
- Institute for Healthy Families (Professional Therapists)
  https://instituteforhealthyfamilies.org
- Janelle Hallman (Therapy for SSA women & their families)
  https://www.janellehallman.com
- Joel 225: Online Support Groups for Those Who Experience Unwanted SSA (Many Languages)
  www.joel225.org
- Positive Approaches To Healthy Sexuality (PATH)
  www.pathinfo.org

Faith Ministries

- Courage / Encourage (Catholic)
  www.couragerc.net
- North Star (Mormon)
  www.northstarlds.org
- Restored Hope Network (Christian)
  www.restoredhopenetwork.com
- Strong Support (Muslim)
  https://www.strongsupport.co.uk
- Transforming Congregation (Methodist)
  www.transformingcong.org
- Wife's support groups
  http://www.brothersroad.org/whj/helpforwives/

Parents & Children's Organizations

- PFOX: Parents and Friends of Ex-Gays and Gays (Christian)
  www.pfox.org
- Support for Children of LGBTQ+ Parents
  www.dawnstefanowicz.org

Other Organizations

- https://www.davidpickuplmft.com
- https://familystrategies.org/our-team/
- https://www.reintegrativetherapy.com
- www.voicesofchange.net

About the Author

Richard Cohen, M.A., is a psychotherapist, educator, and author who travels throughout the United States, Europe, Latin America and the Middle East teaching about marital relations, parenting skills, healing from sexual abuse, and understanding gender identity and sexual orientation issues. Over the past 35 years, he has helped hundreds in therapy and thousands through healing seminars, as well as trained over 6,000 physicians, therapists and ministry leaders how to assist those dealing with gender identity and sexual orientation concerns.

Cohen is the author of 1) *Being Gay: Nature, Nurture or Both?*, 2) *Gay Children Straight Parents: A Plan for Family Healing*, 3) *Understanding Our LGBTQ+ Loved Ones*, 4) *Healing Humanity: Time, Touch, and Talk*, 5) *A Therapist's Guide: Assisting Our LGBTQ+ Loved Ones*, 6) *Rich's Home*, and 7) *Clinician's Handbook: Assisting Our LGBTQ+ Loved Ones*. His books are published in twelve languages.

He founded the International Healing Foundation (IHF) in 1990, and is currently the president and co-founder of Positive Approaches To Healthy Sexuality (PATH). Based in the Washington, D.C. metropolitan area, PATH offers consultations, family healing sessions, resource materials and speaking engagements. Cohen is a frequent guest lecturer on college and university campuses, and at therapeutic and religious conferences.

Cohen holds a Bachelor's degree from Boston University and a Master of Arts degree in counseling psychology from Antioch University. For three years, he worked as an HIV/AIDS educator for the Seattle, Washington chapter of the American Red Cross where he authored a statewide curriculum for foster parents and health care providers dealing with HIV infected children.

Cohen has been interviewed by newspaper, radio and television media including appearances on *20/20, Jimmy Kimmel Live, Rachel Maddow, Howard Stern,* ABC, NBC, CBS, CNN and other news outlets throughout the world. He lives in the Washington, D.C., metropolitan area with his wife of forty-three years and has three adult children.

Positive Approaches To Healthy Sexuality (PATH)
P.O. Box 2315, Bowie, MD 20718 / Tel. (301) 805-5155
Email: pathinfo@pathinfo.org
www.pathinfo.org
www.TimeTouchandTalk.com

www.ingramcontent.com/pod-product-compliance
Lightning Source LLC
LaVergne TN
LVHW021238080526
838199LV00088B/4567